證明奉者懷⼝東輪船同行⼈⼀年有寄月日即到大西巴里京城
並無過犯可謂托賴
天主罷德助保祐不勞招攬執事咸宜難
謝歎一矣豈洲從照相識之⼈事
普住其⼈⼝不如⼝⼝聽而⼝⼝
罷德助殺人令我害怕連日其送會
告白無罪既解之強種上應對⼝
於至西洋五十閏月日約有啟一
封交現住間罪沙㗎東高漢人
手送投 閣讀 示婦期未如到西
自開汉⼝⼿會⼝清水濱堂

The Question of Hu

The
QUESTION
of HU

Jonathan D. Spence

Alfred A. Knopf
New York
1988

THIS IS A BORZOI BOOK
PUBLISHED BY ALFRED A. KNOPF, INC.

Copyright © 1988 by Jonathan D. Spence

Library of Congress Cataloging-in-Publication Data
Spence, Jonathan D.
The question of Hu / Jonathan D. Spence.
p.   cm.
Bibliography: p.
Includes index.
ISBN 0-394-57190-8
1. Hu, John, 18th cent. 2. Converts, Catholic—China—Biography.
3. Foucquet, Jean François, 1665–1741. I. Title.
BX4668.H82S66 1988
909.7′092′4—dc19
[B]   88-21564
                                                CIP

Manufactured in the United States of America
First Edition

FOR
Colin and Ian

Heureux qui, comme Ulysse,
a fait un beau voyage

—Joachim du Bellay

Contents

Acknowledgments

The idea for this book came to me on the night train from Pesaro to Florence. However, I could never have had the idea had I not read—a year or so before—the erudite and absorbing study on Father Jean-François Foucquet, S.J., written by Professor John Witek, S.J., of Georgetown University. Near the end of that study, Professor Witek gives a brief summary of the problems that arose between Foucquet and Hu and it was this that my brain, unwittingly, had retained. When I returned to the United States, Professor Witek's meticulous footnotes led me first to the relevant printed materials and thence to the archives in three countries, while his courteous response to some early queries quickened my resolve to complete the quest. I am deeply grateful to him.

My thanks, too, to many other scholars who replied swiftly to my requests for bibliographic help: Robert Dietle, John Merriman, Natalie Zemon Davis, Emilia Viotti da Costa, Grace Goldin, Theodore Foss, W. J. Bynum, Robert Schwartz, Robert Darnton, Laurence Winnie, Joanna Waley-Cohen, and Peter Brooks. For help in attempting an at least fairly lucid translation of John Hu's distraught letter of 1725, I am sincerely grateful to Ch'en Jo-shui, Chin Annping, Wu Chen-liang, and Yü Ying-shih.

Portions of this book were first presented as part of the Morgan lecture series at Dickinson College in Pennsylvania, in the fall of 1987; others were presented as segments of the Christian Gauss seminars at Princeton University, and of the Lax Memorial Lecture at Mount Holyoke College in Massachusetts.

Isabel Smith helped me with her advice at a crucial stage in the formation of the Charenton chapters. Karin Weng brought typewritten order to the patchwork of my drafts, as Florence Thomas did to my revisions. Both Harold Bloom and John Hollander gave a careful reading to the penultimate draft. To all of these generous people, my thanks.

In pursuit of Hu I traveled to many of the places where he had been before me, to Canton and Bahia, to Port Louis, Vannes, and the Maison Professe in the Marais, as well as to the site of his former hospital in Charenton, now separated by an eight-lane freeway from the dark waters of the River Marne. In all these places I found protective presences, and I would like to thank them here. I would also like to thank the archivists and their staffs who helped me on so many occasions as we grappled with their aging treasures for traces of Hu: in Paris, at the Archives Nationales, the Archives des Affaires Etrangères, the Bibliothèque Ste. Geneviève, and the Bibliothèque Nationale; in Rome, at the Bibliotheca Apostolica Vaticana; and in London, at the British Library and the Oriental Manuscripts Depository. The directors and staff at the Psychiatric Institute and the Hôpital Esquirol in Charenton, and at the Wellcome Institute of the History of Science in London, were similarly helpful.

As with all my previous books, Yale's splendid collections and their keepers hastened my task at every moment. As with all my previous books, too, my wife, Helen Alexander, had to take the full force of the aloneness that always comes over me as I write. For the fourth time, now, Elisabeth Sifton served as my careful and caring editor, with that special enthusiasm that only her authors know. And just in case all that love and caring from so many people might not prove enough, my aged dog Daisy climbed the narrow wooden steps to my summer study countless times a day, and lay across from me during every word, sighing gently in her sleep over my endless attempts to draw some meaning out of the constantly vanishing past.

Preface

Perhaps the most astonishing thing about Hu is that we know anything about him at all. The Chinese biographical tradition is rich in the materials it has preserved on scholars and statesmen, philosophers and poets, men of unusual moral rectitude and recluses distinguished by their eccentricity. Even merchants might be recorded if they were both wealthy and charitable, and soldiers if they guarded the borders with valor or suppressed indigenous revolts. But Hu was none of those things. He was an exasperating and apparently unprepossessing man, who had very little money, no distinguished relatives, and only a perfunctory education that left him equipped for nothing except the copying of other people's texts. He had courage, but no skills in warfare. A convert to Catholicism, he never rose high in the ranks of the Church. And though he did travel once to Europe, in 1722, and stayed there over three years, much of the time in a madhouse, he wrote only two brief letters about his experience, and one of those was lost in transit.

Yet very considerable detail about Hu is now preserved in three of the world's great archival collections: the Bibliotheca Apostolica Vaticana in Rome; the British Library in London; and the Archives des Affaires Etrangères in Paris. The main reason for the survival of these materials is the guilty conscience of the man who brought Hu from Canton to Europe in 1722, the Jesuit Father Jean-François Foucquet. After Hu returned from France to China, in 1726, blurred rumors began to swirl in both Paris and Rome that Foucquet had, in various ways, treated Hu shabbily. Desperate to preserve his good name—he had only recently been elevated to a bishopric—Foucquet wrote a long account of his relationship with Hu and circulated it among a select group of friends and senior churchmen. Foucquet called his account the *Récit Fidèle,* which can be translated as "True Narration." One copy entered the hands of the Duc de Saint-Simon, the celebrated chronicler of the reign of Louis XIV and a friend of Foucquet's, whence it passed with the rest of Saint-Simon's papers to the French National Archives. One copy somehow reached the open market later in the eighteenth century and was given to the British Library by a donor in the nineteenth century. One copy was handed over to the papal archives, along with the rest of Foucquet's unpublished writings, his journals, and his letter books, presumably after his death in 1741.

Each of these three copies of the *Récit Fidèle* has additional marginal notes and author's comments, showing how carefully Foucquet continued to polish and elucidate his own work when he had the time. The copy in France has fewer of these addenda than the copies in Rome or London, suggesting that this was the earliest version, perhaps sent personally to Saint-Simon, whose influence could be expected to help exonerate Foucquet. The British Library copy has inserts of one or two letters not found in the other copies, and extensive marginal notes, but also some lacunae and references to documents "to be inserted later" that are not in fact in the manuscript, suggesting it was an intermediate version. The copy in Rome not only has a few brief explanatory notes not found in the Paris and London copies, showing it was the last of the three to be worked on, but also has an invaluable group of appended letters, labeled "A" to "N," which are full versions of the letters often only summarized or paraphrased in the *Récit Fidèle* itself. In addition, bound in with the Rome copy is the complete run of correspondence concerning Hu, dated 1724 to 1725, that Foucquet had with another Jesuit Father, Pierre de Goville.

Elsewhere in the Vatican collection, preserved along with miscellaneous seventeenth- and eighteenth-century Chinese documents, is the only known writing by Hu himself, a letter in Chinese ideographs to Foucquet that can be dated from ancillary evidence to October 1725. The confidential reports to the Chinese Emperor from senior officials in the Canton region, now stored in the "Number one Ming and Qing Archive" in Peking and recently published in facsimile, though they do not mention Hu by name, give details on the arrival and departures of the French fleet with which he traveled to Europe. They also give considerable information on Louis Fan, the Chinese convert to Christianity who traveled to Europe just over a decade before Hu and returned to China the year before Hu left. Some other pieces of the story can be added from the early files of the Paris police officials and the directors of the hospital for the insane at Charenton. These are preserved in the French National Archives at the Palais Soubise in Paris. A rather garbled version of parts of Hu's story was published in a 1764 issue of the newsletter called *Lettres Juives,* and Voltaire picked up this partial version and further elaborated it in a short passage of his *Dictionnaire philosophique*.

Ultimately, however, it is on Foucquet that we have to depend for our detailed knowledge of Hu. Unlike some modern guardians of our fate, Foucquet did not attempt to prove his own innocence by erasing the past from the record. Instead, he carefully kept and filed away every memo and letter that came his way, even if the material did not show him in a pleasant light. He copied and recopied many such items, convinced that the record in its totality would vindicate his views of his own rightness. I don't happen to think Foucquet was right in the way he treated Hu, but I am only able to make that judgment because he lets me. Thus even if I believe I have confronted him successfully Foucquet remains, in a way, the victor.

J.D.S.

Block Island
Summer 1987

The Question of Hu

1

The Question

Hu stands a moment at the doorway to the reception hall, looking in. The room is filled with about a dozen seated men in clerical robes. The attendants who dressed him and escorted him from his cell wait at his side, in case he should be prompted to some act of violence. They have not told him why he has been summoned, since he knows no French and they know no Chinese.

Hu has spent two and a half years in the hospital for the insane at Charenton, and his clothes have almost all disintegrated. He wears a torn and dirty shirt of Chinese cut, and a pair of underdrawers. His feet, in what remains of a pair of Chinese stockings, are thrust into broken slippers. Round his shoulders he has pulled the remnants of a European jerkin. His long dark hair, uncombed, falls around his shoulders. "His face had the look of an exhumed corpse," Father Pierre de Goville, one of the watching clerics, wrote three days later, "and since he had neither the physical stature nor the kind of face that would help transcend his condition, he looked more like a vagabond or a beggar wracked by hunger than like a Chinese man-of-letters."

When Father Goville calls out a greeting in Chinese, Hu brightens for a moment, as if with some inner satisfaction. But at the same instant he sees, behind Goville, a large crucifix hanging on the wall among the religious paintings in their gilded frames. Pointing to the crucifix, as if the assembled company have not seen it, Hu falls to his knees and prostrates himself flat on the floor five times with his forehead to the ground—returning to his kneeling position after each prostration. His homage paid to his crucified Lord, he stands up again and acknowledges each person in the room with a Chinese bow of greeting, hands folded before his chest. Only then, urged on by the company, does he take a seat.

Hu and Goville talk for more than an hour. Goville speaks Chinese well, for he lived twenty-three years as a missionary in China, mainly in or around Canton. During a period when the English merchants there could find no Chinese willing to serve them as linguists, he acted as their interpreter. He asks Hu the reasons for his near-nakedness, for his poverty, for his lack of any work contract from Father Foucquet, the man who brought him from China in the first place. Hu answers each question volubly and at length. At the last, Goville asks Hu if he has no questions himself. Yes, says Hu, he has one. "Why have I been locked up?"

2

Departure

Hu has been named the keeper of the gate. Father Domenico Perroni made the appointment. Perroni directs the
Sacred Congregation for the Propagation of the Faith,
which on behalf of the papacy coordinates—or tries to—
the work of the various Catholic missionaries in the Canton
region. Hu's job will be to check who goes in and comes out
of the Congregation compound, which contains not only
the residences and administrative offices of Perroni and his
staff but also a sizable church. At times there will be delicate
decisions to make on whom to admit and whom to exclude.
The Cantonese are excitable people, and the Westerners not
always popular.

Hu certainly seems a sensible choice for the post. He is
forty years old, a widower. His wife died many years ago,
leaving him one son, now nearly grown. He never remar-
ried, but lives with his mother and one of his brothers. Hu
was born southwest of Canton, somewhere near the sprawl-
ing commercial city of Fatshan, among the snaking creeks

and canals of the Pearl River delta region, although his family came originally from farther north, in Jiangxi Province, and Hu still refers to himself as a Jiangxi native. Hu is quite scholarly and extremely devout. When one says "scholarly," one means not that he has passed the government's civil service examinations which would ready him for employment by the state, nor that he knows any European languages, but that he knows how to read Chinese, can write it neatly, and has some grasp of classical forms and phrases. He will be able to keep any records that his position might require. This level of literacy is important, for in August a servant of Father Perroni—whose official duties as Procurer-General of the Sacred Congregation in South China inevitably generate a great deal of confidential correspondence with the local missionaries and with Rome—misdirected a crucial letter. The servant took the letter to a Franciscan instead of a Jesuit, because their Chinese surnames sounded just the same although they were written with quite different ideographs. The result was embarrassing, even damaging, because the Franciscans acquired some information they could use to their advantage.

Hu's devotion to the Christian faith, moreover, is well known and of long standing. He was converted back in 1700, when he was nineteen years old, during the time the Jesuit Fathers Gaspar Castner and John Laureati were making such a vibrant base of Christian belief with their preaching and church-building in Fatshan and the surrounding region. At his baptism Hu took the name of John, in homage to Father John Laureati, and when his son was born he had him, too, baptized, as Gaspar, in honor of Gaspar Castner.

Hu's knowledge of Christianity, and the sincerity of his belief, led to his being selected as one of the catechists attached to the church of the Sacred Congregation. Such choices are not made lightly, and the Chinese catechists of Canton have an enviable reputation for diligence and sincerity. Since the Chinese will talk to each other so much more frankly about secret matters than they will to Westerners, the European priests use their Chinese catechists to approach potential converts and seek out their inner doubts and unravel family problems that may be impeding their religious advance. They also scour the streets at dawn, looking for babies who have been abandoned by desperate parents. The babies, usually on the verge of death from disease or malnutrition, are brought back to the various mission compounds where the catechists are stationed, and are at once baptized. If they die soon after, at least they do so in God's grace. If they live, and a Christian Chinese foster family can be located, they can be raised as Christian children. The catechists also have a working agreement with the staff at the hospital for abandoned children, who inform them when a baby is about to die; a catechist can then hurry to the hospital and baptize the infant there himself. (The European Fathers don't dare go inside the hospital, because there are wet nurses on duty at all times, and the threat of major scandal is too great.) Catholics in Canton baptized 136 babies in 1719 and 241 in 1721, though heaven knows how many others had to be left to die where they lay.

Canton is a big city—it takes almost an hour to reach the center by carrying-chair if your house is on the outskirts. The Europeans living there guess the city's population to be around one million, and those who know both cities think Canton is about the same size as Paris, though the buildings are all single-storied, which makes it hard to judge. Canton is really four different cities in one, all of which abut each other. On the north bank of the Pearl River, set back a little from the water, is a walled area known as the "Chinese city," where the governor-general of the region has his Canton office, as does the Emperor's supervisor of foreign trade, the "Hoppo," as the Europeans transliterate his official name. The streets here are narrow and crowded, filled with small shops. North of the Chinese city is a second walled area known, since the Manchu conquest of China in the 1640s, as the Manchu or the "Tartar" city. Most of the Manchu garrison forces live here, and the governor of Guangdong Province has his main office here. With its broad public avenues, many of them paved, interspersed by symmetrically placed and aligned triumphal arches, the Manchu city has a spacious and ordered look, fit setting for the formal buildings where the local officials hold state examinations and perform the solemn ceremonies for Confucius.

West of these two enclaves, the high walls and gate towers of which announce their official status to all visitors, lies a third metropolis, the commercial and residential heart of Canton, with streets paved with slabs of finely laid fieldstone, gracious shops and homes, and the warehouses of the more prosperous merchants stretching along the river bank. In this area, proof of both affluence and a mature sense of comfort, the streets are sheltered with awnings to give protection from the fierce summer sun. The fourth city is one that sprawls along the Pearl River's edge and in the maze of smaller inland waterways and canals. This is the realm of the very poor and the boat people; here boats are moored in serried rows, their crowded masts jumbled against the sky, making "avenues whose trees are ships," in the words of a French observer.

The foreign residents are dispersed in different parts of Canton. In the western suburb, near their spacious European-style church, live the Portuguese Jesuits. In the northeastern part of the Chinese city live the French Jesuits. Between these geographical poles are the churches and residences of the other religious orders and the Sacred Congregation for the Propagation of the Faith. On the river's edge, just south of the point where the western suburb meets the Chinese city, are the lodgings and warehouses of the foreign merchants, which they call their "factories." By shrewd negotiation the French have won from the Chinese officials the right to have a permanent residence here, and their base is prosperous and well appointed. Other countries' merchants and officials—British, Dutch, Ostenders subject to the Habsburg emperors—come and go with the monsoon cycles and the vagaries of international politics.

The long-distance ocean vessels of all these countries—except for the Portuguese, who use their own colony of Macao nearby—anchor ten miles down the river, at Whampoa Island. It is here that their boats are registered, measured for tax purposes, and inspected by the Hoppo's subordinates, and that the bulk goods they purchase for shipment to Europe are loaded. Here too are sheds made of bamboo and matting for drying sails and storing supplies, and open spaces where sick sailors can rest and exercise. The merchants and crew must travel up from Whampoa to Canton on their small cutters or on sampans hired from Chinese boatmen.

The Sacred Congregation is at the heart of all this European life in Canton. Father Perroni is always on the move, visiting other churches, or off in Macao, as he is now so much of the time, arranging various details in preparation for the departure of the papal legate, Carlo Mezzabarba. But even when Perroni is away there is no lack of excitement.

For instance, only last year Louis Fan was here, after his astonishing ten-year sojourn in Europe. Fan, a Catholic convert from northern Shanxi Province, had become the assistant to the Jesuit missionary Francesco Provana. When Emperor Kangxi ordered Provana to Rome on a special diplomatic mission to the papacy, Provana took Fan with him. The two men landed in Portugal and traveled thence to Italy. Fan saw strange cities and inland seas, witnessed miracles; was received twice in audience by the Pope; learned Latin and became himself a priest. When his ship docked at last at Macao harbor—Father Provana, alas, had died at sea, though his body was still aboard in a coffin—the senior military and civil officials of the region reported the fact posthaste to the Emperor. Fan was given an armed guard of imperial troops to escort him on a river boat through the internal waterways that led to Canton. Lodging with the Catholic fathers, he was interviewed by the governor-general and one of Emperor Kangxi's imperial commissioners, and began to write up his memoirs, before being summoned north to report to the Emperor in person.

Even though Fan's adventures may fade to legend, at the Sacred Congregation the outer world remains always present for the keeper of the gate. Besides the Jesuits, there are Augustinians, Franciscans, and Dominicans, and all sorts of visitors from the papal legate's own staff. There are merchants and ships' officers from the French and British vessels at anchor in the harbor, and the directors and staff of the French factories and the state trading company, the Compagnie des Indes.

Hu's horizons open. A vision begins to form at the center of his being: he will travel to Rome himself, and meet the Pope.

MONDAY, 6 OCTOBER 1721.
CANTON

At last Father Jean-François Foucquet is feeling a little stronger. He has been ill in bed since 10 August, and at times he lay near death. What makes this long illness all the more alarming is that he was also sick earlier in the year, on the way south from Peking, after making a winter crossing of the Yangzi River.

Though relieved to have recovered, Foucquet has lost a lot of valuable writing time—almost two months of it. Recently he has been very much aware of his mortality. His letters are filled with references to his being fifty-seven years old and risking the ruin of his life's work just when it seems to be coming to fruition. "Now that I am fifty-seven, a single year, six months even, are infinitely precious to me," as he puts it. He also has considerable reason to feel bitter, for his individualist views have made him unpopular with many of his superiors in the order—often men younger than himself—and he feels they are deliberately interfering with his work.

Technically speaking, Foucquet won't be fifty-seven until 12 March 1722, but he is in his fifty-seventh year, and the minor exaggeration is pardonable, for he has certainly had a long and active life. Born to a prosperous family in the town of Vézelay, in Burgundy, Foucquet went to study at the Jesuit college of Louis-le-Grand in Paris, becoming a Jesuit novice in 1681, at sixteen. In his early twenties he taught mathematics and acted as a tutor to other young boarding students from the provinces. He was ordained a priest in 1693, volunteered for Far Eastern mission work in 1694—he did not specify the country and was drawn to accounts of mission activity in Japan and Siam as well as China—and was chosen for China service by the Jesuits working with Louis XIV's encouragement to strengthen the French presence there. Foucquet reached Amoy in 1699, and served lengthily in Fujian and Jiangxi provinces before being summoned to Peking in 1711 as an expert in the interpretation of the Chinese classic *The Book of Changes*.

In November 1720, Foucquet was ordered to leave Peking and to travel south to Canton at once, by the land route. Although he had been petitioning for years to be recalled to Europe, so that he could get on with his scholarly work in peace, he had never anticipated having to leave in such a rush. Foucquet's superiors in Peking gave him only eight days to pack up all his possessions, his books, and his notes. Even the sixteen mules he hired, loaded down, could carry only a part of his formidable library, and he had to leave more than twelve hundred volumes behind, filled with precious jottings and marginal annotations. Three cases of these were later sent on down to Canton by water but too late to reach him, and mounds of the personal papers he left behind were thrown away and destroyed.

The reason for the haste of his departure, he was told, was so he could have a chance of catching a boat of the French East India Company that would make a winter sailing with a favorable wind. But even though despite his illness and the difficult winter traveling conditions he managed to reach Canton by 20 February, none of the anticipated French ships had yet arrived. So he wasted almost a full year waiting while the ships slowly limped in from various points where they had been forced—having missed the monsoons—to spend the winter.

Foucquet's Chinese books, assembled and repacked, fill eleven crates. That is over and above another seven crates that he has helped to purchase in the Nanjing book markets on account, with money provided by the French East India Company, which are destined for the King's library in Paris. It is his own eleven crates that matter the most to him, for they contain the heart of his researches: the Chinese texts with his interpretations that will prove the mysteries of the true religion and save the mission in China from the errors into which it is falling. There are close to four thousand volumes in Foucquet's eleven crates, and he lovingly divides them according to fourteen basic categories. Pride of place goes to the texts of China's so-called Five Classics, *The Book of Changes* and the other four titles that make up the ritual, poetic, and historical canon. These are followed by editions of Confucius' own *Analects* and the other short works that form the basic curriculum of a Chinese education, along with histories of China's successive dynasties, works on Daoism and language, of general classical commentary and philosophical speculation, on the sciences, government, education, and rituals. Buddhist texts—to be consulted as examples of Chinese idolatry—find their place at the end, along with some general works of exegetical fiction, like the great Ming picaresque novel of a Buddhist priest's travels to India, *Journey to the West,* and a batch of works written in Chinese by various Catholic missionaries. Foucquet's handwritten itemization of his titles alone takes him forty-eight pages.

In the twenty-two years that Foucquet has been in

China, he has given much of his life to proving the truth of three fundamental insights that have been granted to him: first, that the origins of the ancient Chinese religious texts, such as *The Book of Changes,* are divine, that they were handed to the Chinese by the true God; second, that in China's sacred books the word for the "Way"—the "*Dao*"—represented the same true God that Christians worship; third, that the same divine significance could be read into the Chinese philosophical phrase the "*Taiji,*" used in so many texts to refer to an ultimate truth.

To prove the correctness of these views to skeptical, even hostile superiors, Foucquet has to pin each of his arguments down to a specific item in a specific text, and though he uses many, *The Book of Changes* remains the most fruitful. Take, for instance, the Chinese belief that there is a divine force that exists beyond desire, beyond disorder, living in total tranquillity. Each springtime this force chooses to abandon its peaceful withdrawal so as to make things grow for all mankind. In *The Book of Changes,* says Foucquet, one who reads correctly can see this being's desire to come to earth, and the thousand subtle expositions that accompany it, as being intimations of Christ's Incarnation. The Thirteenth Hexagram of *The Book of Changes* clearly tells of the Coming of Emmanuel and the sorrows of a world that has lost its innocence. The Fourteenth Hexagram shows how, for three long years, the enemies on earth will fight against the Lord and resist His laws. The Twenty-fourth talks of the Firstborn, and the Fifty-ninth of the working out of His purposes as the small flock disperses and the larger one is brought home. "At the general reunion of all Peoples," Foucquet knows, "which is clearly foretold in this hexagram, the earliest state of mankind will be renewed, and the first happiness of the world. A great and brilliant light will shine upon all the nations that will recognize the sovereign Lord and submit themselves to Him."

This is Foucquet's work, this is his passion—to make all these things clear, to unravel all the hidden meanings in the Chinese past. "In such an enterprise," writes Foucquet, "the act of labor becomes sweet, and even the harshest pains become in some way delicious."

Yet the act of labor is also time-consuming and desperately difficult. Foucquet has already spent years roaming through all the early classical works and teasing out the clues that led him toward the truth. Just to transcribe the passages can take days, even weeks, when there is so much else to do. For a time, in Peking, Foucquet had Chinese secretary-assistants, who not only helped him by writing out long Chinese passages but also learned to copy his correspondence—in Italian, French, and Latin—by laying a sheet of thin Chinese paper over the original text and tracing it letter by letter, with perfect accuracy, even though unable to understand a single word. In 1718, however, allegedly because use of such assistants violated his vows of poverty, his superiors forbade him to employ any more Chinese. Foucquet believes their real reason was to stop him from bringing his work to fruition.

Despite this prohibition, once he got to Canton Foucquet met two Chinese converts who attended the Jesuit church. They were good scholars, and eager to help him with his work—their collaboration was another of the activities seriously disrupted by his illness. The French ships will be leaving soon for France, and Foucquet with them. Is it possible that he could persuade one of the Chinese to come along? They could go to Paris and on to Rome. There are precedents for that kind of thing, and Foucquet has noted them carefully. Admittedly the only two Chinese in recorded history yet to visit France did not return to tell the tale. Michael Shen, who traveled to Europe with Father Couplet in the 1680s, met two kings, Louis XIV and James II, and did useful work at Oxford, but died at sea on the way home. Arcadio Huang, taken to Paris by Bishop De Lionne in 1714, married a Frenchwoman, had a daughter, settled down to work in the Royal Library, and died soon after from an illness, along with his little family. But Louis Fan is a more encouraging example of what the loyal service of a Chinese assistant for a Western priest can mean, right down to Fan's tenacious protection of Provana's body after his death, refusing to allow his beloved teacher to be buried at sea but bringing his corpse all the way back to China for a Christian burial in sanctified soil. Foucquet was still in Peking when Fan came through the city on the way to the imperial audience. By a strange coincidence the imperial permission for Foucquet to return to Europe—Western missionaries in China may leave only if the Emperor consents—was issued just a few days after Fan had instructed the Emperor on some of the geography and customs of that continent.

And now both the papal legate, Mezzabarba, and Father Antoine Maghalaens, whom Emperor Kangxi is sending on an embassy to Portugal, have decided to take Chinese assistants with them—as Foucquet is well aware. They have made no secret of it, and although the Emperor, for national security reasons, tries to stop Chinese from traveling overseas, there are always some intrepid souls who are willing to go, whatever the possible cost.

SATURDAY, 13 DECEMBER 1721.
CANTON

Domenico Perroni comes to Foucquet's room in the Jesuit residence to bring an oral message from the papal legate: Foucquet now has official permission to take his library to France. Written confirmation will follow later. Only last week Perroni made a similar visit, to bring the legate's instructions that Foucquet is to proceed to Rome after Paris. In Rome, he is to meet with the Pope and inform His Holiness about the general situation of the mission in China.

It is good of Perroni to come in person like this, especially since the streets of Canton have been unusually dangerous lately. One of Scattergood's men from the *Bonitta* killed a Chinese down at Whampoa, and there have been cries for vengeance. Armed Chinese troops have been patrolling the streets, and no foreigners feel completely safe. Their warehouses and residences are being watched. Scattergood himself has gone into hiding, and one can hardly blame him. The last time something of this sort happened, an English doctor quite unconnected with the homicide was seized by a mob, savagely beaten, and thrown down on the ground to die next to the corpse of the dead Chinese. The Chinese garrison commander has already put five men from the *Cadogan* into jail just because they happened to be walking around near the docks—though he released them when the British merchants as a group threatened a total trade closure.

The Chinese authorities have to be watched carefully on these matters and can be very tough. Three missionaries affiliated with the Sacred Congregation were jailed in 1710 on the vaguest of charges and are still under arrest after eleven years, with no formal accusations ever brought against them. One had served the previous papal legate as interpreter, one as a physician, and one had tried to send a gift of wine and medicines to the Emperor without permission—and for these reasons alone they had incurred imperial suspicions and were now wasting their lives away.

Foucquet has missed some of the current excitement because he has been in the French Jesuit residence and church, making a religious retreat to give himself strength for the long journey ahead. It is now definite that the ships will sail in early January.

Though Foucquet, as a Jesuit priest, still lives in the residence for the French Jesuits in the northeastern section of the Chinese city, he has been drawn more deeply into the world of the Sacred Congregation and of those who take orders directly from the papacy. His contacts with the legate Mezzabarba and the orders to go to Rome reinforce the intellectual distancing he feels from the other Jesuits, who will not accept his views on the significance of the religious imagery in the Chinese classics and who hew to an independent line on the Chinese rites, refusing to believe that they are religious in nature. In some circumstances this makes it easier for them to convert Chinese scholars who worship their ancestors, but they are deliberately violating the papal ban on taking such a position. Father Pierre de Goville, procurator of the French mission in Canton, and thus Foucquet's superior although Foucquet is three years older, comes to Foucquet's room on occasion to discuss these problems, and they have lengthy conversations. But Foucquet is more drawn to Perroni, with whom he has formed a deepening friendship that began in June. The two men enjoy talking over ecclesiastical politics, the local forces hostile to the propaganda, the problems facing the papal legate's embassy, and Foucquet's own prospects in Europe.

Some time before the permission from the papal legate came through, Foucquet sent Goville one of the lengthy letters he likes to write, begging for permission to take the books he got out of Peking. He also sought to take with him some other books he had ordered by mail from Europe, which finally reached him on the French boats that have recently arrived. Goville is legalistic about ownership rights, and feels many of the books should be kept in China as possessions of the Jesuit order, since they need a good research library there desperately. He also invokes the vows of poverty to Foucquet, who protests vigorously: "Is this merchandise that I want to carry with me? Am I engaged in trade? Are these books the same as beautiful clothes, or commodities, or luxuries unsuited to my state?" Foucquet is obsessed with the length of the journey ahead of him, and with the need to work on the books during the voyage if he is not to waste precious time. He will even ship the books right back to China as soon as he reaches the dock in France if that will satisfy Goville, he tells him, or give them to some Jesuit house in France.

Goville does not always find Foucquet's arguments convincing. The Chinese texts may be easy to find substitutes for, he responds, but what of all these expensive European titles now arriving? The *Genealogy of the Pagan Gods* by Boccaccio, Tycho Brahe's *Astronomy,* works of Pico della Mirandola, Macrobius, a guide to Greek roots, a twelve-volume set of Lipsius at 28 francs, and a four-volume breviary at 52 francs? And Hoffman's four-volume folio dictionary at an astonishing 122 francs? On the one hand, Foucquet wants reimbursement from the Society; on the other, he wants to take the books with him. He can hardly have it both ways. Goville's ideal is diametrically the opposite; he would like both to make Foucquet pay and to have him leave the books in China.

The legate's permission to ship all his books—or at least those that have reached Canton—given over the head of his own superior, relieves some of Foucquet's nagging worries. But it only increases another: where can he find the Chinese assistant he needs? The two Chinese scholars who attended the Canton church were both interested and would have been perfect choices, he believes. They were personable and clean and had the requisite linguistic skills. They could even make the translations for him, under only loose supervision. With either of them as company on the long journey to Europe he could have maintained proficiency in his spoken Chinese, something only possible with daily practice. But both Chinese suddenly lost interest without giving any clear reason. Foucquet is growing convinced it is because Father Goville talked them out of it.

MONDAY, 22 DECEMBER 1721.
CANTON

Foucquet calls on Perroni at the Sacred Congregation compound. The vessels are due to sail in only two weeks, and he still has found no Chinese assistant. Surely Perroni, with his contacts, can find someone.

It is all especially frustrating for Foucquet, because he has arranged the shipment of his eleven crates of books in the most ingenious way. There are now three French ships at anchor in Whampoa, the *Galatée,* the *Maure,* and the *Prince de Conti.* Foucquet has been tracking their movements with care, since his own passage to Europe depends on their schedules. The *Prince de Conti* and the *Maure* both missed the late monsoons in 1720 and had to anchor a full six months off Hainan island before reaching Canton in May 1721. The *Galatée* was delayed even longer, and had to winter at the bleak and almost deserted island of Poulo Condor off the coast of Cochin China, where there were no natural supplies of food, no game, and where a struggling group of French settlers and soldiers were endeavoring to establish a naval station. The *Galatée* reached Canton only in August, bringing with her many of the dispirited settlers, who abandoned the little shelters they had managed to build on Poulo Condor to the elements and the monkeys. The Chinese authorities in Canton, ever watchful of foreigners' comings and goings, meticulously reported the arrival of the French boats to the Emperor himself. The *Prince de Conti* is reputed to be the fastest of the three and hence likely to reach France first, so Foucquet has arranged with the captain, M. Baugrand, to take him and his Chinese assistant—if he can find one—aboard. With such a speedy ship they should be in France by May or June.

Always cautiously planning ahead, Foucquet has also made a point of getting to know the two key Frenchmen in the Canton financial world, the director of the French factory in Canton under the French East India Company, M. de la Bretesche, and his deputy, Tribert de Treville. Ever since 1698, the Chinese have permitted the French directors to reside in Canton, and, because of their willingness to perform the formal prostrations of the kowtow, they have always been handsomely treated there. Both Bretesche and Treville are from Nantes, whither the goods from China are generally shipped under bond after landing at Port Louis, in Brittany, and they have good connections in China and France. Before leaving France, Bretesche had been instructed to buy up a major collection of Chinese books on the topics of religion, politics, sciences, arts, and language, and the regent of France, the Duc d'Orléans, had provided the foresight for this decision and the cash to implement it. The books were to be bought with money furnished on account through Peking and Manila. Bretesche got to know Foucquet as they worked together to arrange the purchase of Chinese books in the Nanjing markets for the King of France's library. Foucquet drew up a precise list for a major collection, and Bretesche sent a Chinese merchant to go and buy all the books on the list in Nanjing. Either for lack of time, money, or interest, the Chinese merchant bought only some of what had been requested, but even that fraction filled seven crates.

Foucquet and Bretesche have also met quite often at formal dinners, and Foucquet has helped Bretesche—who arrived in China only in mid-May—by giving him a list of translated terms and vocabulary needed to deal with Chinese merchants. Bretesche has reciprocated by sharing confidential information with Foucquet about the Company's future plans for expansion, such as their desire to take over St. John's Island, south of Macao, as a naval base. He also provides fine wine for the Mass, and even loans members of his household staff and his personal silver table settings when the Jesuits want to entertain the papal legate in special style.

The Company's deputy director, Tribert de Treville, vis-

its Foucquet at the Jesuit residence after his business meetings with the Chinese commercial resident, the Hoppo, and
keeps Foucquet informed of all the charges and counter-
charges over the Chinese rituals being bandied about in
Canton, and prepared in Latin and French drafts for dispatch
to Europe. It is Treville who has arranged for Foucquet to
bring a Chinese assistant on board the *Prince de Conti* whenever he can find one, and has also arranged that each officer
and ensign on the *Prince de Conti* will take one of Foucquet's
eleven book crates into his own cabin, so that Foucquet will
not have to pay expensive freight charges. The European
books he just received, for instance, cost 268 francs and the
shipping was 30 francs, and at such a rate of more than 10
percent, the cost of eleven crates would be prohibitive. This
is more than an idle gesture on the part of the officers, for
the goods they take home in their own cabins provide a
huge proportion of their profits from the voyage, and total
four times their salaries for a given tour of duty, and even
more. Foucquet is pleased, for all his books will be safe and
near at hand all the time. Yet without a Chinese to help him,
his triumph will be hollow. Perroni promises to do what he
can to help.

WEDNESDAY, 31 DECEMBER 1721.
CANTON

Foucquet has found a Chinese assistant to go with him
to Europe. He is John Hu, the keeper of the gate at the Sacred Congregation for the Propagation of the Faith.
For more than a week Hu has been watching Foucquet
hurrying in and out of the Congregation to see Perroni.

Foucquet is an inspiring vision, with a truly magnificent beard reaching almost to his waist, and the gleaming robes the Jesuits wear in the China mission—an under-robe of white, a belted blue silk over-robe, a wide-sleeved black tunic, a little conical hat and cloth shoes, a fan in his hand. He has a kindly face, too, and speaks with compelling authority. He will soon be seeing the Pope, people say, and he carries with him the aura of Rome.

Hu hears that Foucquet has been looking for a Chinese assistant for some time without success. He doesn't dare speak directly to Foucquet, but goes to Perroni and volunteers his services. Perroni, confident that he can find another gatekeeper and knowing how soon the ships are sailing, notifies Foucquet. Before talking to Hu, Foucquet asks Perroni if Hu seems reliable and is literate. Perroni says Hu has given no trouble in the three months he has worked at the gate. He shows Foucquet a page of calligraphy that Hu has copied from a Chinese document. It seems serviceable, if inelegant.

So Foucquet interviews Hu. The interview is brief, for Foucquet has only a little time to spare. He is too charmed by the coincidence of Hu's presenting himself at this moment of need to make any thorough test of Hu's literary skills. He finds Hu, whose skin is dark, physically ugly. He is also none too clean and has a despairing look to him, as if he has been reduced to deep poverty from some once more fortunate state. But he is available. He wants to make the adventurous journey. The two men discuss the terms. A deal is made. "It was either this Chinese or none at all," Foucquet writes later.

The two men draw up a written contract and sign it. Hu will serve as a copyist on a five-year term, at the end of which period Foucquet will pay his passage home. Hu's ba-

sic annual wage will be twenty taels (ounces of silver), and
Foucquet will also furnish his food (but no other expenses),
the passage to Europe, and incidentals on the voyage. These
payments are all conditional on Hu's performing his work
as copyist on any of the four thousand books they are shipping on the *Prince de Conti* as stipulated by Foucquet. Hu
requests, and is given, ten and a half taels in advance for his
own and his family's needs. Hu's brother will look after their
mother. Father Perroni will find some work for Hu's son
Gaspar in the Congregation's church.

Foucquet buys several sets of brand-new Chinese
clothes for Hu in the town, along with the various small
personal items Hu will need on the boat, and one of the
highest-quality bed coverlets obtainable—an outer casing
of damask stuffed with fine cotton wadding, which costs
fifteen *scudi* at current Chinese prices. Foucquet offers Hu a
copy of their work agreement to keep for himself, but Hu
will not accept it. What need is there, he says, for his own
copy? He has absolute trust in Father Foucquet. Let Father
Foucquet keep it for him.

Hu is convinced he is going to see the Pope. Foucquet is
a little guarded on this, but does not rule it out as a possibility. He says he will find "honorable employment" for Hu as
soon as they reach Rome, a guarantee he feels safe in making, since the papal legate, Carlo Mezzabarba, just before
leaving made this blanket promise for any Chinese Foucquet might bring, and even put it into writing. Hu also believes that he will be able to write up his travels in the form
of a book that will make him famous among his countrymen
when he returns. Surely he will be seeing astonishing
places, doing amazing things. Foucquet does not contradict
him on this.

As much as possible, their preparations are conducted

in secrecy, since Father Goville has made clear his continuing objections to having Foucquet take a Chinese assistant along with him. In addition to the arguments concerning the Jesuit vow of poverty, and the various objections that Foucquet's own views on religion are too eccentric to deserve any further encouragement, Goville feels there are important legal considerations. In recent years, in Canton, there have been several cases of accidental deaths of Chinese caused by Europeans, and in each case the Chinese authorities have harried the small European community of traders and churchmen until massive restitution was paid. The recent Scattergood imbroglio is a case in point. If a Chinese were to travel with Foucquet, and were to die in Europe, there could be dangerous consequences. The Church's position is fragile enough as it is. "I know this kind of Chinese," says Goville, "and above all I know the people of Canton." These arguments are not without weight, for Goville has been in China for twenty years and in Canton for the last thirteen. But Foucquet has been in China for twenty-two, and is a tenacious man.

MONDAY, 5 JANUARY 1722.
CANTON, WHAMPOA ANCHORAGE

Foucquet and Hu are aboard the *Prince de Conti,* merchantman of around 450 tons, crew of seventy, thirty guns, Captain Baugrand commanding. The sails are hoisted, the anchor is raised, and they are heading out of Whampoa and down to the open sea.

Hu is lucky to be here. Yesterday somebody leaked the news to Father Goville that Foucquet had found a Chinese assistant, and Goville tried to use his influence as Foucquet's superior to prevent Hu from sailing. He called on both directors of the Company, Bretesche and Treville, and asked them to forbid any of the three French ships from taking a Chinese aboard. But Treville in turn leaked that news to Foucquet in a hurried note: "The plot is discovered. M. de la Bretesche has just shown me a letter from Father de Goville, telling him he's recently learned that you are taking a Chinese with you. He begs him not to permit it, especially since he's given his word on behalf of both of them to the mandarins, and this business will cause terrible embarrassment to both him and M. de la Bretesche. Do what you think it best to do. I am completely at your service."

Bretesche does not pass on Goville's message to the ships' captains, and Foucquet arranges for one of the officers to take Hu quietly aboard the *Prince de Conti*. Foucquet boards more publicly, leaving from the French factory, where he had spent the night, with all his own personal possessions: the indispensable Chinese and European books he wants in his own cabin, his dictionaries, his Chinese brushes, a selection of Chinese clothes, his ecclesiastical robes, his underwear, his bonnets, and his small collection of religious medallions.

Spirits are high on the three French ships as they prepare to sail. Each ship carries full cargoes consisting of tea, silks and other fine fabrics, inlaid cabinets, and porcelain specially designed by the Chinese for the export trade. The cargoes' total value on the open market at Nantes is estimated at ten million francs. Profits can be huge on these trips if all goes well, and if they are successfully supplemented by speculation in the gold and silver rates with money given on account to buy merchandise. Changes in the financial organization of the Company, currently being made by Paris financiers, are expected to drive them even higher.

None of the officers on the *Prince de Conti* seems to mind the eleven crates of Foucquet's Chinese books that crowd their cabins, and they welcome Father Foucquet aboard, in his clerical robes and flowing beard. Appreciatively he lists their names in his *Journal,* after that of Captain Baugrand: Guillebart, second captain; Motte and Balbeder, lieutenants; Duvandie and Mottay Bossinon, ensigns. They seem equally welcoming, too, to his Chinese assistant Hu, resplendent in his smart new clothes, with his gleaming black pigtail, and an expensive damask coverlet to keep him warm on the winter ocean nights.

3

The Ocean Voyage

No one has gone anywhere yet. For eight days there has been no wind and the three ships have drifted only a few miles downriver with the tide, on the sluggish gray-brown waters of the delta, under the lines of barren hills.

Foucquet is writing letters—to Goville, to Perroni—and making fair copies, from the rough drafts of letters already sent, for his files and his journal. He and Hu have not yet developed a full work plan for the long months ahead, though Hu has done a few hours of copying Chinese books under Foucquet's guidance.

Life on the *Prince de Conti* is comfortable if monotonous. At least they are not lying there in the heat of the summer sun. Foucquet gets on well with the officers, and the Frenchmen all dine together. Hu, however, is not asked to join them. He is seated with an intermediate group, which includes Captain Baugrand's major domo and the various personal domestics of the ship's officers. In terms of economic status, this is doubtless correct, since Hu's annual salary of twenty taels—equivalent to eight French francs a month—is less even than the wages of a common seaman on the ships of the Compagnie des Indes, the youngest of whom can expect nine francs at the least, the veterans fifteen to eighteen. But if Hu is aboard as a scholar, perhaps he should be with Foucquet and the officers and ensigns, for their number is traditionally swollen to include the ship's scrivener and the chaplain. Even if their salaries are far higher—scriveners getting as much as fifty francs a month, the chaplains thirty—their jobs are no nobler than Hu's; he is after all the hand-picked copier of precious Chinese texts.

Hu has learned no word of French yet, and his dining companions speak no Chinese. The Frenchmen murmur together that Hu seems to have little idea of how a European meal is served; he just takes whatever he wants as soon as it appears on the table. His companions try to explain the idea of portions to him. It is not an easy concept to convey, and Hu continues to eat more than they feel he should. They occasionally use a measure of force to restrain him.

WEDNESDAY, 21 JANUARY 1722.
OFF THE COCHIN COAST

The island of Poulo Condor is just ahead. The winds came up, at last, on 13 January, and the three ships passed by Macao, without stopping, on the 15th. Since then it's been a straight, clear run, with the monsoon winds from the northeast.

Foucquet is invigorated; it is wonderful to be on the move at last. This is "the happiest possible kind of navigation," he writes in his *Journal.*

Hu is not eating with the major domo, nor with anyone else. He is not doing any copying, either. He is being desperately, violently, consistently sick.

This has proved to be a dispiriting landfall, though for someone as sick as Hu the mere act of being at anchor must bring some solace. Two French Jesuits are on the island, Jean-Baptiste Jacques from Lyons and Antoine Gaubil from Toulouse. Both are trying to get to China but have been stuck here for four months with the ship that brought them, the *Danae,* while the future of the little colony the French are trying to establish is clarified. Jacques finds Poulo Condor a "terrible place to live." Gaubil calls it "one of the most horrible places in the world."

The island is damp, mountainous, unhealthy. Worms infest the water of the pleasant-seeming harbor and destroy the wood of small boats, and entry to the port is dangerous, through rocks and heaving currents full of sharks. Insects are thick in the air, and sickness endemic. In the forests, monkeys and strange flying lizards abound, but there is no natural edible game or fowl, and one has to live by fishing.

The several hundred local inhabitants are not friendly, and, growing nothing themselves, they move back and forth between the island and the Cochin mainland. The English had a trading base here twenty years before, but after many of the settlers were killed by the locals—in alliance with soldiers the English had hired from other islands to serve as their garrison force—the remainder decided to abandon the island. The French are having no easier time of it. When the

Danae's men moved ashore, several were taken ransom and were rescued only with difficulty.

It has been a nightmare for the French soldiers and German mercenaries posted here—and for the wives whom some of them brought along—living in makeshift huts under the driving rain, trying to persuade the locals to sell them a little food or to fish for them. They have been hungry for weeks, and seize eagerly on the flour, beer, and meat brought by the *Galatée*.

Foucquet talks to Gaubil and Jacques of astronomy and China and the papal legate Mezzabarba's visit. They give him letters that their ship brought him from France. Foucquet, in return, promises to deliver several letters they have written when he gets home. Jacques is not at all well and having serious problems with his eyesight. The conversation flags. Hu does not join them.

Captain Baugrand, along with the captains of the *Galatée* and the *Maure,* discusses the future of the little colony with the two King's officers who were appointed to develop it. All agree that Poulo Condor is simply not a viable base of operations. The decision is made to emulate the British and abandon the island.

Though it means jamming many extra people onto the already crowded ships, the colony's officers, soldiers, and the few family members are loaded aboard. The *Danae* and her crew, along with Jacques and Gaubil, will have to wait until June, when the monsoons change, to continue on their way to China. The other ships, in convoy, will resume their journey to France.

But first they will go to the Dutch territories in Java to try to make some money. The opportunities there sound too exciting to be missed, and rumors are flying of huge profits that await them. Since 1718 both the Dutch trade with China and the Chinese junk trade with the Dutch have been stopped on orders of Emperor Kangxi, in reprisal for the Dutch merchants' attempts to force down tea prices in China. The French ships can surely exploit the situation.

THURSDAY, 5 MARCH 1722.
IN THE INDIAN OCEAN

The *Prince de Conti* is on her own. The *Galatée* and *Maure* are gone. The trouble came in Java, in February. All three ships entered a promising-looking bay together, but it must have been the wrong one. They found no one to trade with, and not even supplies to replenish their stocks, only some fugitives from other villages and the abandoned huts of those who once lived here.

The ships upped anchors and prepared to leave the bay, the *Galatée* and *Maure* leading, the *Prince de Conti* close behind. As the first two vessels edged round the point, the wind in the bay suddenly dropped; the first two ships forged ahead under a strong wind while those on the *Prince de Conti*, watching them grow smaller, were driven back deeper into the bay by strong currents. Captain Baugrand had to drop anchor to avoid being driven onto the rocks. For the whole of the day remaining, the ship's crew labored slowly toward the bay entrance by warping on the anchors. It was futile, and they had to spend the night in the bay. The next morning they sailed out easily, with a fresh wind, but the other two ships were gone.

Hu is still seasick. Foucquet has never known anyone to be sick so badly for so long.

LATE MARCH 1722.
APPROACHING THE CAPE OF GOOD HOPE

Hu has been in a fight with one of the French sailors. The sailor certainly hit Hu, though it is not entirely clear if Hu was able to strike him back. The blows came after some sort of argument flared up and the sailor believed Hu had insulted him. Perhaps Hu did, for ever since he got better, in mid-March, he has been censorious of the loud ways and uncouth manners of the soldiers and sailors aboard.

The blows seem to have made him pensive. Also, one of the crew was flogged publicly and brutally on the bridge for some misdemeanor, while Hu watched with the others. That made him even quieter. Hu seems to think the same thing might happen to him.

MONDAY, 30 MARCH 1722.
ROUNDING THE CAPE

Powerful winds are forcing the *Prince de Conti* along at a terrific pace, a hundred to a hundred and fifty leagues a day, but far to the south of the Cape of Good Hope. The currents combine with the wind to keep them on this wrong course, and there is no hope at all of making a landfall on the Cape for water or supplies.

The seas are dangerously high, and the wind has snapped one of the masts. They seem to be around the 36th degree of latitude and still moving south. They should be far nearer the coast of Africa if they are to round the Cape and catch the currents northward, especially if they hope to make St. Helena and refit there.

MID-APRIL 1722.
THE SOUTH ATLANTIC

The *Prince de Conti* has missed St. Helena altogether. They probably sailed past it in the night, writes Foucquet, or else they never managed to work far enough north to get on the right parallel of latitude.

The ship is almost out of fresh water, and food is running low. Many of the soldiers and crew have scurvy, and the disease is spreading rapidly.

Captain Baugrand, unsure what to do next, calls a conference of all his officers. They decide, after much debate, to try to make the Bay of All Saints, in San Salvador, Brazil. That, given the prevailing winds and currents, is the nearest practicable anchorage. As things stand, without such a landfall they have little chance of reaching Europe alive.

SATURDAY, 9 MAY 1722.
BAY OF ALL SAINTS, BRAZIL

A cannonball smashes into the rigging of the *Prince de Conti*. Captain Baugrand orders the guns run out and the fire returned. In the smoke and noise it is hard to tell what is happening. They are being attacked by a pirate ship that is trying to cut them off from the channel to the Bay of All Saints and drive them out to sea again, so that they can be fought to a standstill and boarded.

Earlier in the afternoon, when the two vessels first sighted each other, there was an attempt to communicate without bloodshed. The other ship ran up a Portuguese flag and the *Prince de Conti* a French one, and officers tried to hail each other. But no one on the *Prince de Conti* knew enough Portuguese to understand what was being said by the enemy, and apparently nobody on the other vessel knew French.

The *Prince de Conti* is outmanned and outgunned. Captain Baugrand can count on fewer than seventy men from all his company who are fit enough for combat should it come to boarding, and he has less than thirty guns. The Portuguese ship has fifty-six guns and appears to have several hundred armed men on board. But Baugrand and his officers decide to fight it out. They can expect to lose everything if they meekly surrender.

It is beginning to grow dark, and a driving rain is falling, mixed with patches of fog, so the enemy ship keeps appearing and disappearing. Captain Baugrand orders all available weapons brought up from below and laid out on the upper deck, so that as many crewmen and sailors as possible can be ready to repel boarders. Hu sees the men take up their weapons and himself seizes a cutlass. Waving it in the air with menacing gestures, he marches proudly round the upper deck, a small figure, fierce as he can be in the gathering twilight.

Through a gap in the fog Captain Baugrand sees that the way to the Bay of All Saints lies suddenly open. Turning the ship about, he speeds for the harbor and, safely avoiding the dangerous rocks that line the island of Itaparica on the port side, he reaches the sheltered anchorage under the guns of the protecting fort of San Salvador. To everyone's surprise, the pirate ship follows and anchors nearby.

Messages are exchanged with the shore, and the riddle is explained. The pirate ship is not a pirate after all. It is a coastal patrol vessel of the Portuguese viceroy, on detail to protect the harbor. Since foreign merchant ships could be expected to call in Brazilian waters any time between October and April on their outward voyages to the Indies, but never in May, the captain of the Portuguese patrol boat had concluded that it was the *Prince de Conti* that was the privateer.

WEDNESDAY, 20 MAY 1722.
BAY OF ALL SAINTS, BRAZIL

The *Prince de Conti* lies at anchor in the Bay of All Saints. Beyond the narrow strip of beach and the scattering of buildings and warehouses that line the docks, a cliff rises sheer into the sky. Neatly spaced along it are the towers and spires of the imposing city of San Salvador, seat of the viceroy and capital of Portuguese Brazil. So high is the city above the sea that three huge winches have been constructed to lift the goods needed by the people up from the wharves below.

It is early winter here in Brazil, but the fields and hills are green around the city of San Salvador. Surely fresh fruit and vegetables, unsalted meat, pure water are all abundant. For the French crew, too, the beauty of Brazilian women is legendary. Ships have been known to delay their sailings for weeks for the sake of the city's sensual delights, leaving only when they had to, with exhausted crews.

But at the moment, all that Hu and the Frenchmen can do is dream about the land. Angry at their firing on his coastal patrol vessel, and unconvinced that the *Prince de*

Conti is not a privateer, the viceroy of Brazil who resides at San Salvador, Vasco Fernandez Cesar de Meneses, has forbidden anyone to go ashore until his men have checked out every inch of the ship. Meneses is a stern man, with an iron will, and not even the sick have been allowed to land. The supplies requested by Captain Baugrand have not been delivered. There is no surcease from the scurvy, and several men on the *Prince de Conti* have died.

On the urgings of the Jesuits of San Salvador, the viceroy makes one exception to his ban on going ashore: Father Foucquet. Foucquet has been allowed to lodge in the Jesuit College, where twenty-four fathers and brothers are in residence. He has already been there for one whole week. The hospitality is overwhelming, and his Jesuit colleagues will not take payment for anything. They give him time for reading and for quiet conversations in his borrowed room. He gets some writing done.

One delightful coincidence—Brother Charles de Belleville is at the Jesuit residence. Belleville—painter, sculptor, architect—reached China in 1698, one year before Foucquet. He designed and supervised the construction of the Jesuit residences in Peking and Canton, in both of which Foucquet lived, and his religious paintings decorate several Chinese churches. Recalled to Europe in 1707, he was transferred to San Salvador in 1710 to continue his graceful work. He and Foucquet have a hundred things to talk about.

The gardens of the Jesuit residence lie along the cliff top, filled with flowers and cacao trees. The Jesuit church, faced with white marble brought from Europe, stands next to the residence, rising high above the central square of the city. In niches over the three massive rectangular doors stand the images of the order's three most powerful founding fathers: Ignatius of Loyola, Francis Xavier, Francis Borgia. Above

them, five tall windows admit the eastern light and illumi-
nate the dark wooden carvings and the softly shining silver
ornaments. At the western end of the church is the sacristy,
a place of especial beauty, where disparate elements fuse
together, the richly painted ceiling lightened from below by
the radiance of blue and yellow floral tiles. Through the low
yet generous windows of the sacristy the eye travels easily
further west, down the cliff and across the waters of the bay,
to where the *Prince de Conti* rides at anchor under the Brazilian sun, with her captive crew of sick or dying sailors, and a
solitary Chinese man named Hu.

SUNDAY, 31 MAY 1722.
OFF THE BRAZILIAN COAST

The *Prince de Conti* sails out of the Bay of All Saints. The
viceroy has finally relented after his men could find no trace
of illegal cargo in the ship's holds; he has allowed supplies
to be loaded, the mast to be repaired, and the French officers
and crew to go ashore. By then they had been on board in
the harbor for fourteen days, and eighteen of the sick had
died. Plans for departure were hurried, and they have not
taken on as much food and water as they might have
wished. It turns out that the Brazilian winter is a bad time
for obtaining food. Ants eat up most of the vegetables
that the locals try to grow, and the only fresh produce
available in bulk consists of oranges and bananas, which
rot swiftly in the ship's hold. As to the meat, mutton seems
unavailable, chickens are scarce, and the beef is of inferior
quality.

Foucquet rejoins the ship just at the last minute, escorted to the dock by his friends. He is relaxed and rested

from his visit, and eager for the last stage of the journey. He now must prepare Hu for what lies ahead.

LATE JULY 1722.
MID-ATLANTIC

For almost two months the winds have been contrary, and progress has been slow. June and July are not a good time for crossing the Atlantic from southwest to northeast.

Hu is calm, but he has grown very thin. There is a new docility in his manner. He makes tea for Foucquet without being asked, and also prepares the ship's little altar for Mass when necessary. On occasion, Father Foucquet lets him assist during the serving of the Mass itself.

Hu has had a vision, he confides to Father Foucquet. His mind was filled with angels, Hu says, angels calling to him. They told him it was his special task to seek out the Emperor of China and introduce him to the truths of the Christian religion. The angels did not think the task would be hard.

Foucquet tries to deflect Hu from such thoughts by telling him of European life and manners, of the kind of things he can expect to find when he lands in France. This way the shock will be less great for him. Foucquet is worried that Hu does not appear to be listening.

MID-AUGUST 1722.
OFF LA CORUÑA

It seems hardly possible, but the *Prince de Conti* is running out of food again, and fresh water, too, is dangerously low. The crossing from Brazil that should have taken forty-five days at most has taken more than seventy, and they have only reached the northwest Spanish harbor of La Coruña. The authorities there won't let them land to take on more supplies, since there has been an outbreak of the plague in Marseilles and a warning is out against all French ships. It does not matter to the Spanish commander that the *Prince de Conti* has been nowhere near Marseilles or the Mediterranean.

They ride at anchor outside the harbor, prevented by a contrary wind from sailing north, prevented by the Spaniards from landing.

As he does when worried, Captain Baugrand calls a council. This time he includes Father Foucquet in the deliberations. In the midst of their discussions, apparently having guessed the subject of debate, Hu comes to the door and interrupts. He stands there and calls out to Foucquet, in Chinese, to come and hear what he has to say. Hu has a plan: "Give me a lifeboat in which I can sail to the town," he says to Foucquet. "I will persuade the governor to listen to our needs. I will make him grant us permission to come ashore, and to buy those things we need to live."

Foucquet tries quickly to dismiss Hu, but Hu will not be quieted. He raises his voice and repeats his offer. He adds reason to reason as he elaborates his argument, crying out that those on the ship have rights, and that he will force the Spaniards to understand that they must be respected. As his words pour forth, the French officers ask Foucquet what Hu is saying. When Foucquet explains, trying to tone down the arguments somewhat but keep the sense, the officers are surprised and amused.

Hu is not allowed to carry out his plan. Instead, Captain Baugrand decides to buy what few supplies the Spaniards will agree to bring to the ship and then to beat up the coast and head for home, hoping for the best. Foucquet begins to wonder if Hu is sane: he broods about the fight, the cutlass, the vision, and now the lifeboat. If Hu is not sane, Foucquet will have to decide what to do.

Foucquet does not know much about Chinese madness, but he ran into one case when he was serving in Jiangxi, twenty-two summers ago. One young woman and eight young men were affected, and Foucquet studied their symptoms and wrote about them to a correspondent in France, using the young woman—she was seventeen or eighteen—as his exemplar: "Physically she seemed perfectly well, drinking and eating with a good appetite, overseeing the business of the household, and behaving in quite an ordinary way. But when one least expected it, she would be seized by a violent fit of madness, during which she spoke of things far off or nonexistent, as if they had been present before her and she had seen them with her own eyes." The young men, who had the same symptoms, had to be tied up at times, lest they hurt themselves or their families. All were cured eventually, by placing crucifixes in their homes and sprinkling them with holy water, but it was a baffling and unsettling experience.

In any case, the parallels between Hu and this other Jiangxi family are far from precise. It has been a long journey. Doubtless, being on shore at last will calm Hu down.

THURSDAY, 27 AUGUST 1722.
PORT LOUIS

The voyage is over. Last night they knew they were close to France, but had to anchor offshore. As soon as it was light, Captain Baugrand made for the Isle de Groix. There, when the news spreads that a ship is back from the East or West Indies, a crowd of small boats always gathers, with Breton crews who know every cove of the coastline, to unload whatever cargo the officers and men have brought for their own private use, before they can be inventoried by the King's revenue officers. Such cargo can be collected inland later, and make a man's fortune. But the heavily armed patrol boat of the Compagnie des Indes was there too soon. One of their customs officers boarded the *Prince de Conti* with ten or so guards. All small boats were prevented from coming alongside. Hatches and storeroom doors were secured, officers' cabins inspected and contents sealed, and the ship with her escort was taken to her designated anchorage in Port Louis, under the shelter of the citadel's heavy guns. The guards are still aboard, scattered around the ship at different points.

From the deck, Hu can look across the bay to France, to the sturdy rows of stone houses with slate roofs, to the prosperous-seeming wharves, to the sloping line of rocky beach, to the thickly wooded promontory to the north.

Down below, Foucquet is writing a letter to his Jesuit superior in France, Father Orry, summarizing the entire journey. The brightness slowly fades from the shore, and one by one the lamps are lighted in the little town.

4

Landfall

In the early morning, a director of the Compagnie des Indes, M. Lestobec, came aboard the *Prince de Conti* and repeated the orders against taking anything off the boat. He also warned against anyone going ashore illegally, though he did not enforce the prohibition on Captain Baugrand and the other officers, who were allowed to go to Port Louis for the noon meal.

Foucquet spends his morning writing another long letter, this time to Abbé Bignon, the King's librarian. It has occurred to Foucquet that Bignon, with his royal connections, might be able to speed the clearance of his eleven crates of books through the lengthy inspection process of the Compagnie des Indes. The sooner that is done, the sooner Foucquet can get on with his great work. To get Bignon's support, Foucquet must convince him that the work is indeed important and that the stakes are high: "It was twenty-three years ago," writes Foucquet, "that I began to study spoken and written Chinese, with the intense desire of finding some way to get inside the written relics of that nation. The style of those books, the ideographs in which they are written, their great age, the subjects that they deal with, all of these are things of which in fact we have no other examples even among the most learned nations elsewhere in the world. All this piqued my already lively curiosity, and I can assure you I omitted no means that might enable me to satisfy it. After many years of incessant study I began to see a sure way to enter into these mysterious depths, which for so long had seemed to me inaccessible. The more I advanced the more I discovered there true marvels, and at last I became convinced that these written relics are like a sanctuary of the most venerable antiquity, yet one unknown in Europe until this present time."

Bignon, Foucquet feels it not too extreme to say, with his wisdom and interest in the Far East, must be a chosen vessel of Providence to advance this great work. Together he and Foucquet could draw into daylight that inner core of blurred truth, "hidden by the holiest of the Patriarchs more than eighty centuries ago under the surface covering of these profound and mysterious hieroglyphs. For that is the true understanding that we must have of these Chinese written characters considered from the point of view of their origin."

The most delicate part of the letter is how to persuade Bignon to use his influence on Foucquet's behalf. Foucquet decides to put it this way: While Bignon awaits the next batch of books to be bought in China by Bretesche, and shipped to France for the library, perhaps he could make temporary use of Foucquet's own eleven crates: "I dare to offer you a few thousand volumes that I have collected with care," as Foucquet modestly phrases it. If Bignon is intrigued by the loan offer, perhaps he would like to borrow Hu as well. Foucquet makes the suggestion casually but clearly: "A Chinese, who knows how to write and who has some abilities, made the journey with me. He has been promised a respectable job in Italy, but perhaps, if someone wanted to keep him in France, he would agree to it without making difficulties. The help of the Chinese is necessary for the explication of their books, and at the very least they can be of great use in making transcripts and extracts from texts, and in hunting up specific passages."

Foucquet has finished and dated but not yet sealed the letter when there is a commotion on the *Prince de Conti.* The royal launch has been sent to collect him! It is startling news, until the sequence of events that led up to its dispatch has been unraveled. When the ship's officers went ashore that morning, they lunched with a senior official of the Port Louis bureaucracy, Etienne-François Renault, who for two years has been chief of procurement of naval stores for the Company fleets. During the meal, they mentioned the presence of a Father Foucquet on their ship. By coincidence, Renault knows Foucquet well; indeed, they traveled together to India from Port Louis on the same ship, the *Le Bon,* twenty-four years before, as each began his service in the East, Renault at the French factory in Chandernagore and Foucquet in the China Mission. Renault at once uses his official prerogative to order the royal launch with its master and crew of four to row out to the *Prince de Conti* and summon Father Foucquet to his home. Foucquet must be Renault's guest; he shall not stay on the boat another day.

Foucquet is startled yet delighted by the invitation. In truth, he and Renault became dear friends on that lengthy, dangerous journey long ago. The trouble is, what should

Foucquet do with Hu? Hu knows nothing yet of European ways. Perhaps he would be an imposition, an embarrass-ment to Renault. Once Foucquet is in the town of Port Louis, he can hunt at leisure for nice lodgings for Hu, some-where that will make Hu feel comfortable and at home. The launch waits, there is no time to thrash out the niceties of the argument. Foucquet has been on the *Prince de Conti* for more than eight months, and there is no Jesuit residence in Port Louis or in Lorient. He must make some sort of a de-cision about what to do. He steps into the royal launch and heads for shore, carrying the letter to Abbé Bignon with him. He has not had time to discuss its contents with Hu.

Hu is left on the *Prince de Conti* with the crew and the watchful guards. There is now no one on board who can speak Chinese. The afternoon passes. Foucquet leaves Hu there, alone with his thoughts, as a second summer night descends. For a few moments the sound of drumbeats drifts across the sea. It is the musicians of the garrison beating the retreat, as they do at every sunset.

SATURDAY, 29 AUGUST 1722.
PORT LOUIS

Hu is at Commissaire Renault's home after all. Fouc-quet's scruples have proved unnecessary. Renault has a nat-urally generous nature, and as soon as Foucquet mentioned that he had brought a Chinese assistant with him on the ship, Renault insisted that he be brought to live with them the next day.

Foucquet went to get Hu this morning. While he was back on the ship, he managed to persuade one of the cus-toms officers—it took gifts of tobacco and alcohol—to let him remove some personal effects and, more important, the catalogue of the four thousand volumes stored in his eleven crates. It is out of the question, as yet, to remove the books themselves. They are bonded by the Company's inspectors, and where or how they will be stored and checked over has not yet been decided. Foucquet's letter to Abbé Bignon, offering a loan of the books along with Hu's services, has been delivered to the post chaise, and perhaps royal influence will be used. The other seven crates of books he purchased with Bretesche almost a year before in Canton arrived in July aboard the *Galatée,* which reached Port Louis two full months ahead of the *Prince de Conti.* Those seven crates have been sent on their way to the King's library, as the Company dares not delay their delivery.

Foucquet returns with Hu and the book lists to Renault's house. Hu is given a room to himself, on the second floor. He will take his meals with Renault's housekeeper, a woman in her fifties. Renault himself is not married, and she has long managed all domestic matters for him in Port Louis.

Hu finds the room stuffy and the bedstead too high. He takes the mattress and the straw palliasse beneath it and puts them on the floor. He opens the window. When the servants see this, they replace the mattress on the bed frame and close the window. Hu returns the mattress to the floor, and reopens the window. The silent struggle continues until Renault's staff give up. Hu sleeps henceforth on the floor, the late summer breeze around him.

In one other way Hu disrupts the rhythms of Renault's household. He refuses to eat with Renault's housekeeper. He will not allow her near him. He makes faces at her, and gestures her away, or simply turns his back whenever she appears. At each meal he does the same. Finally his meals are served to him alone, in a room she does not enter.

TUESDAY, I SEPTEMBER 1722.
PORT LOUIS

Renault is well connected in Port Louis. Though he has only been there a little more than two years, his job of overseeing the procurement and distribution of naval supplies puts him into a hundred lines of business. He knows the bakeries that make ships' biscuits, the barrel makers and the owners of safe, large cellars who enable wine to be stored until ships sail, the dealers in sardines, oil, vegetables, meat. All these goods must be bought and stored by Renault and his staff, while others look to munitions and naval supplies.

Many holders of Renault's job have lived in the bigger shipbuilding town of Lorient or in the business town of Scorff, but he is among those—they are not rare—who prefer the amenities and the prettiness of Port Louis. Through Renault, Foucquet meets the local merchants as well as those in the army and the service of the Company. Today he is dining with the leading figure in the town, the King's lieutenant and commander of the citadel, François Burin de Ricquebourg, a man of forty-eight from Picardy, whose son has entered the Society of Jesus. Foucquet has also met the captain of the port, Paul Bigot, and dined with Louis Martin du Parc, a former ship's captain, now marine commandant of the town. Parc—coincidentally—is locked in a bitter tussle with Ricquebourg concerning jurisdiction over the returning merchant vessels that anchor at the Isle de Groix. Then there are directors of the Company, local priests, and even those whose only claim to Foucquet's attention is that they have pretty gardens in which he can rest awhile.

If Foucquet is moving in such wealthy circles, he must

get Hu a suit of European clothes. Port Louis is a prosperous town, though small, and there are at least a dozen tailors
to choose from, not to mention other mercers and cloth sellers. Foucquet is feeling generous, and chooses an excellent
tailor. He orders for Hu a complete suit of finely woven,
sturdy cloth, for autumn is not too far away, with a tight-
fitting over-tunic, or *justaucorps*. The suit and the *justaucorps*
are of dark brown—"coffee-colored," as people are beginning to learn to call it, now that mocha coffee is becoming a
popular drink in France.

Hu is full of curiosity about the town of Port Louis and
has begun exploring it. He walks around in his new clothes,
gazing at everything carefully, as if preparing material for
that memoir he has told Foucquet he wants to write. He
is particularly fascinated by the big coaches on which
the French embark for their long-distance journeys. The
coaches can't maneuver through the steep narrow streets of
central Port Louis, full of potholes and paving stones at
crazy angles, but they can be found in the tree-lined square
by the inn and by the main gates to the town. Hu borrows
paper and makes several sketches of the coaches. He also
spends an hour or two on Foucquet's texts, but seems too
preoccupied for more than that.

WEDNESDAY, 2 SEPTEMBER 1722.
PORT LOUIS

Hu stole a horse today. Or borrowed one, according to
your point of view.

It happened very quickly. He was standing at his sec-
ond-floor window, looking down into the courtyard below.

Someone on an errand from the countryside rode into the courtyard, for Renault's house is one of the spacious ones in Port Louis, with a large coach door through which one can bring a horse quite easily. The man tethered his horse and went off on his business in the household. Hurrying downstairs, Hu untied the horse, climbed on its back, and was off, around the town.

Hu has never ridden before, but soon he has the hang of it. The streets of Port Louis, too steep and winding for coaches, are grand for lone gallopers—one can ride all round the town below the ramparts, so beautiful to look at yet so impractical for fighting, with their high, narrow ledges where two defenders cannot pass each other and where the recoil from an arquebus could easily send one toppling backward onto the ground below. One can clatter through the narrow streets where the eye is always drawn, through gaps in the houses, to the sea below. One can find a burst of speed in the open training fields below the citadel, whose starlike wings project dramatically out into the water, and where the tide tugs at the pilings on the narrow bridge that connects the fortress with the town. Or through the arches placed in the ramparts one can ride out along the narrow line of beach, or gallop down the tree-lined avenue of the rue de la Pointe, where wealthy merchants trading to the East have their homes.

Hu rides for a long time, and when he does not return, the horse's owner has to run around the town to find him. Scolded, Hu is not contrite. He asks Foucquet why, if a horse is being left unused, may someone else not use it?

The people of Port Louis start to call Hu "Don Quixote." Foucquet wonders if perhaps he should not even wait for Bignon's response but send Hu home right away. He makes preliminary inquiries, but is told this is not the time of year at which the Compagnie des Indes dispatches vessels to China. You do not get rid of Hu as easily as that.

WEDNESDAY, 9 SEPTEMBER 1722.
PORT LOUIS

Hu has done no more riding, but he has done little copying either. Foucquet estimates that Hu has worked, in all, around six hours since landing. It is hardly thus that he will earn his wages.

A letter for Foucquet arrives from the King's librarian, Bignon, written in Paris on 4 September, replying to Foucquet's 28 August shipboard letter. Bignon thanks Foucquet for helping Bretesche to buy the seven crates of books for the library (Bretesche had found the time to mention Foucquet's role in a letter written just two days before the three ships left Canton) and thanks him for his offer of Hu. "You have acted perfectly in bringing with you a native Chinese, who without doubt is a literatus from the way you speak of him. He will only attach himself to me if we can make him stay here—he'll certainly do much better for himself here than he ever could in Italy." It is Bignon's overall goal, he adds grandly, to make the study of Chinese as common and feasible in France as that of Arabic is currently.

Bignon is presiding over a Chinese library of growing splendor. Up until 1697 the French crown had only four Chinese books, a gift from Cardinal Mazarin earlier in the reign of Louis XIV. A further forty-nine Chinese volumes dealing with language and natural history were sent via Father Bouvet to the King by Emperor Kangxi in that year. In

1700, Father Fontaney gave the King a twelve-volume Manchu-Chinese dictionary. In 1708—the precedent would have been chilling to Foucquet if he knew of it—fourteen more boxes of Chinese and Manchu books were given to the King by the controller of customs. The boxes, bound some in blue satin and some in yellow damask, contained one hundred thirteen titles in all. They had been impounded by the French royal customs inspectors fifteen years before and never claimed by their owner. The same year Louis XIV added three more volumes, found in a palace cupboard—two were on Chinese astronomy, written by Western missionaries, and one an illustrated Chinese life of Christ. On receiving his royal appointment as librarian in 1718, Abbé Bignon presented a few Chinese titles of his own, and the following year he transformed this mélange into a major collection by acquiring eight hundred volumes of Chinese books from the Seminary for Foreign Missions. Bretesche's seven crates—bought with Foucquet's aid following guidelines laid down by Bignon's colleague, the orientalist Etienne Fourmont—contain 1,764 volumes in all. No wonder Bignon is interested in Foucquet's eleven crates and the four thousand Chinese volumes that repose in them.

Foucquet responds at once. If his own eleven crates will be of service to Bignon's great venture, then he can only be sympathetic, though his own plans are not yet firm. The matter of Hu, however, needs clarification. "The Chinese who made the crossing with me is not a literatus of the first rank, he is not even a graduate. But he can write and he has been reading all his life. He is forty years old. I will have the honor of presenting him to you and if you think he can be of some service to you, I will suggest to him that he stay in France, pointing out the advantages to him."

Foucquet's scheme might be the making of Hu. As Foucquet knows full well, Arcadio Huang, a Chinese scholar who was brought to France by a Catholic priest twelve years before, settled in Paris and worked in the Royal Library with diligence; he also married and had a daughter, before illness swept them all away in 1716. Bignon, too, knows the precedent of Huang. Had Huang lived, all the inventory of Chinese books would long ago have been cleared. Perhaps with Hu and Bignon at the helm, France's Chinese library will reach new heights of glory in Europe.

TUESDAY, 15 SEPTEMBER 1722.
PORT LOUIS

Foucquet has been too distracted by his own duties and his books to take much notice of Hu. He has sent to Bignon a complete catalogue of his book crates, and an elaborate explanation as to why there are personal possessions along with European books scattered through the crates. There is also a twelfth case he'd forgotten about, full of miscellaneous items. He is worried that the Company's inspectors will think he is trying to bring in illegal goods. The clergy are not immune from prosecution. Thirteen years before, the Abbé Jouin, chaplain of the *Confiance,* had been jailed for four months in the Port Louis citadel on charges of smuggling silver in barrels and crates delivered to the home of a friend, and for having cheated the ship's scrivener out of his share of the boat's profits.

Foucquet has petitioned the officers of the Company— in vain—to be given permission to open up the crates still stored in the ship and to dry them out, for they have been damaged in transit, and he knows some of the books are damp. The Company has ordered all the crates shipped un-opened to their depot in Nantes, where Foucquet himself will have to clear them through customs. Foucquet reserves two seats on the coach for himself and Hu for the coming Thursday.

Hu has been exploring Port Louis more thoroughly. He seems to have observed far more of the town than one might expect, in particular to have seen below its prosperity to those who live in misery—the examples are everywhere for those with the eyes to see: the laid-off soldiers, the sailors who drink up their pay on landing, the children whose fa-thers never come home, the syphilitic men and diseased prostitutes, the amputees from the hospital near the citadel, the night-soil carriers staggering under their heavy buckets of human waste. Hu in his coffee-colored *justaucorps* is a grand-looking fellow by comparison.

When Foucquet tells him they are booked out of Port Louis on a private coach, Hu says he does not want to go. He is adamant. He wants to be a beggar. He wants to walk all across France, begging his way. He wants no coach and horses. His feet suffice. Foucquet is perplexed, but believes that Hu's desire to walk across France may be somehow connected to his desire to write a travel memoir about his experiences. There is no time to humor Hu on such a matter, and in any case it is too dangerous. New laws on the arrest and transportation of healthy vagrants have been promul-gated at Court, and if Hu is picked up by the police he might be shipped off to the French colony of Louisiana, or some-where even more perilous. They have to get to Nantes and clear the books on their way. Ignoring Hu's complaints, Foucquet confirms the reservation.

5

In the Provinces

Foucquet has hired a nice carriage, a comfortable, light two-seater with a folding top. Renault and his household come to see them off. At first, Hu still refuses to make the journey. But suddenly he changes his mind, and the two start on their way. One of Renault's retainers rides along beside them: he has to go to Vannes on business in any case, and Renault has instructed him to stay at their side and keep an eye on Hu.

The tidal coves and mudflats between Port Louis and Riantec yield to gentle hills as they move inland on the road to Merlevenez. There are glimpses of the sea off to the right, through gaps in the firs that line the fields. The road climbs steadily, under great trees cloaked with ivy and drooping clumps of mistletoe, the ditches deepen, and the tangled hedges rise higher above the carriage, closing off the view. The hedgerows are filled with late summer berries.

Hu jumps from the moving carriage and runs down the

road along the hedgerows. He seizes fistfuls of the unknown fruits and crams them into his mouth. He runs through a gap in the hedge into the fields beyond. Renault's retainer rides after him and brings him back. Moments later Hu is off again, and the scene is repeated. And again. It seems that nothing will stop Hu from running, nothing will keep him in his seat.

They will never get to Vannes like this. Their progress has slowed to a crawl. Hu laughs aloud when Foucquet shouts at him to return. When the retainer tries to force him back to his seat, Hu throws himself to the ground and lies there, flat against the earth. The retainer raises his whip and beats the prostrate Hu.

Hu climbs back into the carriage, and sits quietly. They travel onward for three hours, for four, through Merlevenez with the view back toward the River Blavet; up the hill to Nostang, where a huge vista opens up across the country-side to the northeast; across the bridges that span the top-most end of the tidal creeks that reach almost to Landevan, and turn right, onto the main road that runs from Brest to Vannes.

On the main road, they stop at an inn for lunch. A beg-gar, standing outside the inn, moves toward the little group to ask for charity. He goes up to Hu and stretches out his hand. Before anyone realizes what he is doing, Hu takes off the coffee-colored *justaucorps* of his brand-new suit and gives it to the beggar.

Foucquet shouts at Renault's retainer to make the beg-gar give back the coat. Obedient to this order, the retainer strikes at the beggar with his whip. The beggar offers up the jacket, but Hu won't accept it, shouting in turn that he will never take it back, that he will never wear the coat again. No one can make him change his mind, and the beggar is finally allowed to keep his prize.

After lunch, they make the long stretch down the main road to Auray and thence to Vannes. The retainer is watchful, but Hu makes no more attempts to leave the carriage. He sits silent, in his shirtsleeves and vest. So they travel, through the afternoon and into the evening, with the sound of wheels and hooves against the road. Before them, in the city of Vannes, above the crowded houses on the hill, the cathedral rears its colossal bulk into the darkening sky.

SATURDAY, 19 SEPTEMBER 1722.
VANNES

The Jesuit College in Vannes is a beautiful place to stay, and the rector, André Goujet, and his fellow Jesuits make Foucquet warmly welcome. There are in fact two Jesuit institutions, side by side, north of the marketplace and just outside the main wall of the town. There is the college itself, run by the Jesuits since 1629, the first main center of higher education for southeast Brittany, lavishly endowed by local nobles and by Kings Louis XIII and Louis XIV, with its own handsome church completed in 1678. And there is the four-story building—once designed as a seminary to train students for the college—now run as a religious retreat for all those who wish to come.

The two buildings are the focus for the religious life of Vannes, more so even than the cathedral and its chapter. The college attracts more than a thousand students, though these are nonresident, living nearby in lodgings around the market square or in the rue St. Yves. The retreats, which are held twice a month, each for a period of eight days, attract up to two hundred men. (Retreats for women are held at the Convent of the Ursulines, not far away.) All are welcomed, priests and laymen, though treated in deference to wealth and rank. One small wing has only extensive private suites for the wealthy. The two lower floors of the main building have seventeen private rooms per floor, off a central corridor, for those who are used to a reasonable degree of comfort. On one side of the third floor are rows of little rooms each with two beds, for those with little to spend; while for the truly poor, across the corridor, there are long rows of simple pallet beds, each touching its neighbor.

The food for the retreatants, served in the refectory from a central kitchen, is similarly categorized. One can pay as much as six francs eight sous for eight days of meals, or as little as two francs and ten sous. For the larger sum you eat, in one day, three meals off good crockery: bread, fresh butter, wine, soups and stews of beef, mutton, or veal, desserts and salads, substituting fish and eggs for meat on fast days. The cheaper menu consists of soup in earthen bowls and plates of stew. For the very poor, who can afford no meals and have to bring their own food with them, a separate little room is set aside. There are many in this category—simple artisans, students, farmers from the countryside—and their local origins are taken note of in the charter, which lays aside money for a Breton-speaking priest to hear the confessions of "good simple folk who understand French badly."

Hu seems happy here. He behaves calmly, and assists Father Foucquet at the serving of Mass. Father Foucquet gets Hu a new set of clothes—though not this time an expensive one. He asks one of the Brothers in the Jesuit College, who serves as tailor for the community, to have a suit made up for Hu of coarse unfinished cloth.

Foucquet is immersed in his plans for the future, which have grown extremely complicated. Letters, forwarded on from Port Louis by Renault, confirm orders from his Jesuit superiors in France that Foucquet is to report to the Jesuit College of La Flèche, on the Loire, and not to proceed to Paris. Yet at the same time he has the instructions that the papal legate Mezzabarba gave him in China—still kept secret from the other Jesuits—that he proceed to Rome. He has none of his eleven crates of books, which have all been shipped to Nantes. He has promised to see Bignon in Paris. And he has Hu.

Foucquet pours out his worries in three letters, one to the King's librarian, Bignon, one to the King's confessor, Father Linières, and one to the papal nuncio stationed in Paris, Monsignor Massei, to whom all messages from the Sacred Congregation in China are routed. As he tells Bignon, one of the greatest problems seems to be financial. The Jesuit headquarters in Paris is not wealthy, and does not want to pay for his protracted residence, especially since there is Hu to look after as well. And the cost of living in Paris is so high that Foucquet cannot afford to pay for an extended stay himself. If Foucquet himself does have to go to La Flèche, he tells Bignon, he will be happy to let the librarian have Hu.

MONDAY, 5 OCTOBER 1722.
NANTES

Things are not going well in Nantes, where Hu and Foucquet have been for more than a week. It seems impos-

sible to make any progress with clearing the crates of books
through the directors of the Company, even though Foucquet has been given the name of the director he's to work
with and has traveled out in person to the Company depot
at Sesines, several miles from the center of Nantes.

Nantes, in fact, has never been especially hospitable to
the Jesuits. All their first efforts to found schools or colleges
there were stymied by the townsmen and the cathedral
chapter, who preferred members of other religious orders.
When, in 1663, the townsmen finally yielded to the express
instructions of King Louis XIV, and gave permission for
Jesuit buildings to be erected, it was only on condition that
they never teach the central curriculum of belles-lettres, phi-
losophy, or theology, that they run nothing more complex
than a "hospice," and that they buy property only in the
outer suburbs, not the center of town. The large house and
garden in the center of town—in which Hu and Foucquet
are now living—was a clever evasion of this ban, bought
for the huge sum of 40,000 francs through dealers in Paris,
working with names of intermediaries. And though the
Jesuits also cleverly bypassed the clauses concerning the
forbidden subjects by developing classes in navigation,
mathematics, and hydrography, figuring that a major base
of foreign trade and exploration would always have a de-
mand for such skills, the certificates they handed out after a
two-year course were not accepted by the French naval officers, who insisted on retesting the candidates themselves. In
1715 the annual stipend to the professor of navigation—his
students, by deliberate choice, had been drawn both from
the ranks of youngsters just out of school and from veteran
sailors seeking to advance themselves in the world—was
withdrawn by the estates of Brittany, and the courses were
now only being sporadically offered. In these depressing

circumstances, the number of Jesuits in the residence rarely exceeds ten.

Hu has turned sullen again. He refuses altogether to assist at the Mass. He has told Foucquet there are too many women in the church, and that he is offended by this. In obedience to Chinese custom, the Jesuits in Canton did not allow women to attend the services there; nor did the Chinese even allow women to stroll openly in the streets. But Hu has been a month and a half in France by now and should be getting used to French customs, Foucquet feels. In case he should behave wildly again, Hu is being kept within the house and gardens—spacious enough, yet still confining—of the Jesuit residence.

Foucquet has been continuing his correspondence with Bignon. The librarian wrote graciously on 24 September to say he would try to help with Foucquet's expenses in Paris, if money were the main problem. "And as for your Chinese, you will give me pleasure if you send him to me; we will see to his support, and if he can be of some use to us I will see if we can't find some means to keep him here. Be so good as to take up with him all these matters, as seems suitable to you."

Foucquet at last raised the subject with Hu, as he told Bignon on 29 September: "I've sounded out the Chinese about the journey to Paris, and I've found that he expresses some repugnance at being separated from me. Nevertheless, he may change his mind, and if I can't bring him myself, I will do what I can to have one of my friends take him, who will then present him to you."

In that same letter Foucquet unburdened himself to Bignon, using the librarian's question about shortage of money as the entry point to elaborate on his fears that unnamed enemies were trying to undermine his life's work. "To respond precisely to the question you put to me, I do not believe that it was the poverty of the Maison Professe that influenced—or at least influenced much—the resolutions not to call me [to Paris]. I see other motives lying behind the decision. I can't yet be as clear with you about that as I would like to be. But I certainly feel that I can tell you that the Chinese texts have their great enemies, both in China and here. The books' partisans and their defenders are not very agreeable to that sort of people. Herein, if I am not mistaken, lies the real motivating force that sent me an order which will deprive me, at least for some time, of the honor and pleasure of speaking to you about these ancient monuments. If I had your ear, I would have various things to add, but a letter does not allow me the same liberty."

On 3 October, writing to Massei, the papal nuncio in Paris, Foucquet is more direct and more distraught about the trap he is in: "I have with me a Chinese whom I should not have brought." Going to La Flèche would be a disaster for their relationship, yet Hu "ceases to be reasonable as soon as I touch even lightly on the necessity for a separation that will keep us apart from each other, however much I tell him of the advantages that would thereby accrue to him." What could one do with Hu? "He is very difficult to take with one, he knows no European languages, indeed he knows almost nothing of our ways; I am the only one he can understand and by whom he can be understood. This does make it excusable that he should refuse to go either to Paris or to Italy unless I am accompanying him." But Hu has not proved to be good company, and is not easily thwarted in his will, he is not a "docile" man. "His natural inclination, of which I have had many experiences on this journey, has proven to me that if you try and force him to do something the result will be outrageous behavior which I must avoid in any way possible."

The tension of the situation is growing too great for Foucquet to handle. The papal nuncio wants Foucquet to keep the fact that he is headed for Rome a secret, yet he cannot resist the order to go to La Flèche unless he reveals that countermanding order to go to Rome. On 5 October, Foucquet makes his decision. He writes to the French provincial of the Jesuit order, Jean Bodin, and tells him of the opposing commitment he has made.

The same day, although it is only forty-eight hours since he last wrote to him, Foucquet pens another letter to Massei, the nuncio, without letting him know he has written to Bodin. He confirms everything he said in his last letter and repeats a good deal of it. With Hu at his side in La Flèche, open at all times to the persistent questions of his Jesuit confrères, everyone would learn of Mezzabarba's instructions and the whole Roman story would be out. "Even if I were free from this Chinese," Foucquet hurries on, all the world would still know the background to the story.

The words are neat and clear on the paper in front of him: "Even if I were free from this Chinese . . ."

TUESDAY, 20 OCTOBER 1722.
NANTES

Foucquet and Hu are leaving Nantes at last. Foucquet has booked seats on tomorrow's public stagecoach for himself and Hu. They will travel along the Loire Valley to Angers and Tours. From there they will proceed to Blois, to Orléans, and so to Paris.

Foucquet is exhausted. The eleven crates of books are finally cleared through the Compagnie des Indes and on their way by sea to Le Havre, but at great cost in time and energy. He has written fifteen letters in twelve days. Half of them were overtaken by events, crossed with someone else's, or ended up contradicting themselves. And the number of people brought into the negotiations has increased prodigiously.

Bignon's request to the Company commissioners that they send the crates of books directly to Paris unopened— even though coming from the director of the King's library—was not enough in and of itself. The commissioners insisted on going through every crate themselves, despite the extensive damage this caused to the crates, and Foucquet has had to make at least six journeys to the Sesines depot to see to the inventorying. Nor were the commissioners helpful in making sure the crates were waterproofed when resealed, or covering them over from the rains, or even mending the shattered planking.

The King's confessor, Linières, alerted by Foucquet, got in touch with Cardinal Dubois, the King's new secretary of state. Though it was now too late to prevent the thorough inspection being made by the commissioners, Dubois could and did order the crates officially sealed after the inspection, and shipped by sea up to Le Havre and thence by river to Paris. To ensure that there be no tampering, he ordered that they be delivered directly to the lieutenant of the Paris police, Marc Pierre d'Argenson. Despite his modest-sounding title, the lieutenant of police is the head of the whole security apparatus in Paris, and makes weekly visits to Versailles to consult directly with the King and the secretary of state. Foucquet's affairs are now being handled at the highest levels. Dubois has also written to D'Argenson, telling him to deliver the crates to Foucquet when he reaches Paris. Foucquet would prefer to have the books travel by the Loire Valley route, as the English Channel is stormy at this time of year and the danger of further damage—even of loss through shipwreck—is considerable. But the Loire route would be far more expensive, and anyway matters have been taken out of his hands. At least he, Hu, and the books can all leave Nantes.

Linières has also suggested a solution to the problem of Hu, if Foucquet needs a release from this "embarrassment." Father Armand Nyel, a veteran of the China Mission, back in Europe for seven years and now in Paris, is returning to China by the first available boat. "He will be happy to take the Chinese with him, if it turns out to be too much trouble to keep him, as I can foresee that it will be."

But Foucquet and Hu still have to get to Paris if such a transfer is to be made. That trip at least is now definite. Foucquet need never have written to Bodin at all, on 5 October, admitting the deal he had made with Mezzabarba, for Bodin had already decided to release him from the order to report to La Flèche and to allow him to come to Paris. These were two of the many letters that crossed.

And Hu? Hu is in a strange state, sequestered in his ample garden. He still refuses to copy anything. The sole result of their nine months' collaboration, notes Foucquet sadly, is a slender notebook of copied documents that most people could have made in a day.

While Foucquet was saying Mass one morning, the superior of the Nantes residence, Father Aumaître, happened to look out of the window into the garden. Hu was kneeling there, his hands reaching up toward the sky, his face contorted, uttering strange cries. Nobody in the residence could understand what the gestures meant or what Hu was trying to say.

TUESDAY, 27 OCTOBER 1722.

BLOIS

The trip between Nantes and Blois is not a success. Hu is like an unbridled horse, says Foucquet, galloping around the countryside as he did on the way to Vannes. Whenever he sees anything new to him, he must leap out and look at it. If there's a windmill, he must climb up onto it and study its construction. Things were difficult enough when they had their own rented carriage. Now they are in the public stagecoach, and all Hu's actions take place under the public's astonished gaze.

To try to check Hu's forays, Foucquet buys him seats at the back of the carriage, away from the door and windows. But Hu shows remarkable skill in persuading other passengers, by gestures and by looks, to give up their seats near the door. Once there, it's only a matter of time before the door is open and he's off. One evening, as night approached and they feared not reaching the next stage, the passengers and some passers-by tied Hu by a rope to the coach and let him run along behind them. That quieted him for a while, and when released he stayed in his seat till they reached the inn.

Every meal is something of a trial for Foucquet. Hu seems unaware that kitchens are off limits, and goes everywhere he chooses, taking things to eat that he fancies from tables and from cupboards. When the staff objects, he shouts back at them—imperiously—in Chinese. A crowd of the curious gathers. There are tussles, blows. Once, Hu seizes a knife in his defense.

Foucquet tries to explain in advance, if he can, what people should expect, but Hu cannot always be anticipated. Some days he refuses to sit with Foucquet but demands his own table, and has Foucquet give him money so he can order his own meal himself—by signs. When the weather is cold, Hu, already dressed in stockings and two sets of drawers, stations himself before the inn's main fireplace and lifts both tunic and shirttails to warm his backside.

Foucquet doesn't see how he can take Hu with him to the main Jesuit house in Paris. There will be scandals, which he at all costs is anxious to avoid. His books, his researches, his life in Rome are all in the balance. In such straits one turns to friends. He can think of two he likes and trusts, Fathers Jean-Baptiste du Halde and Léonard Gramain. Du Halde was a young instructor at La Flèche when Foucquet taught mathematics there in 1696; now he is personal secretary to the King's confessor, Linières. Gramain, one of the friends of Foucquet's youth, a man who sent him money all through his China service so that he could buy more books, is now rector of the Jesuit College in Orléans.

Foucquet is decisive when he needs to be. He writes to du Halde, and asks him to find private lodgings for Hu in Paris. And he books two places on the coach to Orléans, to throw himself and Hu temporarily on Gramain's mercy.

TUESDAY, 3 NOVEMBER 1722.
ORLÉANS

Foucquet has left in the night for Paris, without a word to Hu. Foucquet believed that if he'd told Hu he was leaving, there would have been scenes and chaos. Hu, awakening to find Foucquet gone, is astonished and alarmed. Father Gramain manages to explain, by signs and gestures, that Foucquet will soon be sending for him.

Hu likes and trusts Gramain. He likes Orléans. He is content to wait here, in the spacious Jesuit residence with its vast walled garden, and its lofty church. Hu spends a good deal of time inside the church, which is enriched with two large pictures. One, by Simon Vouet, is of the seated Virgin. The other, by an unknown artist, is of a terrestrial globe, upon which stands the Lord in His glory. The Lord is flanked by four emblematic figures, each one of whom personifies one of the four quarters of the world.

6

Paris

Hu's fears seem all assuaged. At Foucquet's request, Gramain put Hu on the coach from Orléans to Paris, and he made the journey without incident. Hu loves Paris, that's the main thing. He loves everything about it, the noise, the bustle, the height of the private houses, the magnificence of the churches, the quays along the Seine, the palace of the Louvre, the grand bridges, the public squares. "It's a paradise," he tells Foucquet one day, "it's a paradise on earth." Hu doesn't often say things like that.

Paris is in a particularly festive mood this November, because of the public celebrations in honor of the first communion of the young King Louis XV, and of the impending declaration of his coming of age, which will slowly move him away from the regency of his uncle the Duc d'Orléans, and into ruling in his own name. The Jesuits of Paris earlier put on a grand ballet in honor of the occasion, in a Chinese vein, showing allegorically how the sage Chinese rulers of the past chose their own heirs on the grounds of their wisdom and virtue rather than just on birth. And in the last few weeks there have been several imposing displays of fireworks and other illuminations—some of them also centered on Chinese motifs—that have lit up the French night sky.

But perhaps this sense of well-being stems also from the house where Hu is staying. He is lodging with the Bayneses, an English Catholic family. It was Father du Halde who arranged the whole thing, within a couple of days of receiving Foucquet's letter from Blois. James Baynes was an officer of the deposed British King James II, and followed him into exile in France. After James's death, Baynes stayed on in Paris. He is married, and has a daughter around twenty. They've arranged to take in Hu at full *pension*—bread, wine, soup, and meat dishes plus a private bedroom. In fact, they are feeding Hu at a quality 20 sous a day higher than that for which they are charging Foucquet. Foucquet had originally hoped just to find someone who would keep Hu for a week, but the Bayneses imposed no time limit on their offer and have given Hu a "suite of rooms that would suit a gentleman of quality." Baynes has been told by du Halde that Hu can be eccentric, but that rest and good food, perhaps a little medicine, should soon cure him. Du Halde has not mentioned that Hu can be violent. In fact, du Halde is not himself sure on this, since Foucquet has been rather evasive on the matter.

Du Halde's own view is that Hu's strange fits are mainly attributed to a bodily indisposition brought on by the sudden change of food and climate. If medical help were needed, there is a Jesuit doctor coming to Paris soon, bound for the China Mission, whose skills are sure. Du Halde is a little worried that whoever takes in Hu may "get his nose bloodied," but he shares those worries only with Foucquet. Also, du Halde is nervous that Foucquet's secret departure from Orléans might have panicked Hu, left with no one who could understand him. But that fear seems to have been unfounded. The Bayneses don't talk Chinese, of course, but that doesn't seem to bother Hu. His only odd behavior is that he has pulled all the bedding and the mattress off the big bed in his room and insists on sleeping under the open window, but the family accept that. He has plenty of warm coverlets and seems to wrap himself up well.

The Bayneses' house is right behind the Maison Professe of the Jesuits, between the rue St. Antoine and the river Seine, so that Foucquet can check occasionally on his assistant. But mainly he's too busy, and Hu is left to explore nearby on his own.

The Maison Professe is the headquarters of the Jesuit organization in Paris, and there is more than enough for Hu to explore right there. The cluster of buildings and gardens, assembled from a succession of royal gifts and shrewd real estate purchases, is backed against the old city wall of medieval Paris. The main building is made glorious by two enormous paintings of Melchior Gherardini: one, four stories up, which can be viewed through the central axis of the spiraling staircase, shows St. Louis in his glory; the other, on the ceiling of the library in the north wing, shows various scenes representing the evangelization of the world by the Jesuits. The books in the library are rare and varied, over twenty thousand in number. The collection is built around three generous gifts made to the Jesuits between the 1680s and 1720. Crowds of the curious come to view the display, and to study the prints of the martyrs and the illustrations for every saint's day of the year. There is a collection of rare medallions, too, donated by the previous King's confessor, and a host of rare and scientific curiosities given by various donors: an ostrich egg, a chameleon's skeleton, a stuffed bird of paradise, a rose of Jericho.

More than thirty priests are in residence here, and twenty Brothers. Nine special staff look after them—a porter, tailor, baker, cook, refectory head, purchasing agent, sacristan, apothecary, and doctor—and these nine have their own subordinate staffs of servitors and assistants. The budget of the establishment is some fifteen hundred francs a month when you add up all the costs of olive oil and bread, wine, fuel and meat, coals, and candles—and all the other extras that make life glide by a little easier: pipes, chewing tobacco and snuff, for instance (to the scandal of some), hot chocolate and coffee, the use of rented carriages. In this one building, Hu can view the universe of France in miniature.

Only steps away from the Maison Professe is the church of St. Louis, the religious heart of the Jesuits in Paris. Fallen somewhat from its seventeenth-century days of glory— when huge crowds thronged the church each week to hear the greatest preachers in Paris, and one of the major items in the church budget was for extra chairs and for washing out the mud and dust that poured into the church each day on the boots and shoes of the faithful—the building is still magnificent, with its generous dome and the ornate front bordering on the rue St. Antoine, embellished by three massive doors, the gift of Cardinal Richelieu himself.

In front of the church is the fountain built in 1707, one of the engineering wonders of a changing Paris, since it is fed by a powerful pump near the Nôtre-Dame Bridge on the river Seine, and is itself so constructed that the water pressure is high enough to send the flow of water throughout the neighborhood, where it is needed most.

It is only a short walk south to the river Seine, past the Convent of Ave Maria. There a little wooden bridge on stilts leads to the island of Louviers, where piles of firewood are for sale, and boats dock to sell fruit and hay. Along the riverbank, before the spacious public gardens of the Arsenal, is a stretch of open ground where, under rows of great trees, the people play at croquet with their rented mallets. If one tires of that spectacle, between the island of Louviers and the island of Nôtre-Dame is the little port of St. Paul, where larger river craft unload their wine, along with lime and lumber, cobblestones and coal. Water coaches leave from here for Burgundy and Auxerre. The long-distance land coaches for the same destinations and for Lyons also leave nearby from the Hôtel de Sens. The five-arched bridge Pont Marie, lined on both sides with multistoried houses, links the northern shore with the island of Nôtre-Dame. Moored by the bridge are the floating boat-shops for freshwater fish, where one can make a purchase almost any hour of the day or night.

East, Hu can stroll down the rue St. Antoine, here at its widest point, past the church of St. Paul to the right and the formal avenue to the magnificent Place Royale on the left, to the three huge arches of the Porte St. Antoine, with its curious angular spires at each side. To the right of the gate rise the eight tall rounded towers of the Bastille behind their ramparts, to the left in the long ditches of the old ramparts crossbowmen and arquebus men practice their shooting.

Straight ahead, past the foundling hospital, through the flat countryside, on which a few grander houses are now beginning to rise, stretch the dusty vistas of the road to Charenton.

While Hu explores, Foucquet, as usual, has a hundred things to do. He has to see the papal nuncio about the details of the journey to Rome, and to confirm his plans with Father Tamburini, the general of the entire Society of Jesus, who resides in Rome. And he's been having lengthy discussions with both Father du Halde—who is deeply interested in China—and Father Nyel, the missionary allegedly leaving soon for China who Linières had said would be happy to take Hu back with him if that proved necessary. Nyel in fact has changed his plans, and does not seem to be going to China, not at the moment anyway. He and du Halde pump Foucquet concerning his exact views on the Chinese rites and the significance of Chinese classical writings. Foucquet knows that they will pass on his explanations to Rome, since his views are seen by many as eccentric and controversial, and he answers fully and carefully. The Chinese lack the key to their own classical writings, he explains, because that key is the knowledge of the Christian mysteries. Other Christian missionaries in China, of course, did know the Christian mysteries but did not realize that they provided the key. Hence they could not understand Foucquet's views.

As to the Chinese ancestral rites, says Foucquet, though many Jesuits would like to think these are ethical acts rather than religious practices, the Pope has declared them superstitious and therefore Foucquet accepts that judgment. Yet Foucquet shows he is aware of the subtle ambiguities in this whole question. He has met many intelligent Chinese who did not believe the souls of their ancestors resided within a specific set of tablets. For example, a family whose members were dispersed in different parts of China could all worship their ancestors at the same time even if they were in different locations. It was the ancestral spirit rather than the tablet itself that gave force to the ritual. Foucquet believes the Chinese rites will eventually be accepted by Rome as constituting merely a civil and political cult. Such a decision would not contravene Foucquet's fundamental conviction that in the long-distant past the Chinese had worshipped the Christian God. During Foucquet's time in China, it was clear that the Emperor's own public ceremonies had grown distinct and separate from all ceremonies performed by the common Chinese people. Foucquet's special contribution, he believes, lies in his having found a compromise position between the Emperor and the Pope that could satisfy both and reopen the way for Christianity to be spread in China.

Foucquet's thoughts are all on Rome, to which he has been ordered to proceed with all due speed, and in his mind he goes through every possible plan to get there. Though the Marseilles plague has been declared officially over, and the bishop there has ordered all the churches reopened, the lingering effects of the plague still make a southern sea journey from Marseilles, or one over the southern Alps to Piedmont, impossible. Foucquet checks the more northerly land route by coach via Strasbourg and makes two tentative reservations for himself and Hu. But his eleven crates of books have not arrived at Le Havre, and he does not have a valid passport yet for the journey. Only Secretary of State Dubois can issue that, and he seems to be in no hurry. There is one other possibility. When the books do reach Le Havre, Foucquet could send Hu there, and join them later; then he and Hu and the books could all go together by sea, by the English Channel and the Strait of Gibraltar, avoiding the plague zone, and landing perhaps at Livorno. Foucquet sounds out Hu on this latter plan. Hu of course does not know all the geographical details, but he seems delighted at the thought that they might soon be on their way to Rome, and that he will at last be able to see the Pope.

Foucquet has no time to guide Hu around Paris, but Father Orry, coordinator of the French Jesuits in the Far Eastern missions, offers to take on that task. Orry is interested in Hu and wants to see him happy. He deputes one of his secretaries to take Hu all around the city, to all the spots a foreigner might find interesting. They have fixed the outing for Friday, 27 November.

FRIDAY, 27 NOVEMBER 1722.
PARIS

Hu must be lost. He has not come back to the Bayneses' house. Nobody knows where he is.

As planned, Father Orry's secretary met Hu this morning at the Bayneses', and took him off sightseeing. They had reached the west side of the Tuileries Palace and were enjoying the spectacle there, when some sudden shift in the crowd of sightseers, some momentary lapse of attention, swept the two men apart. The secretary looked everywhere, but could find no trace of Hu. He had to return alone.

The Bayneses were worried and alerted Foucquet. Foucquet was anxious too, and left a message for D'Argenson, lieutenant of the Paris police. (D'Argenson lives not far from the Maison Professe, on the Vieille rue du Temple, so it was not hard to leave the message for him.) D'Argenson in turn alerted the Archers of the Watch, who patrol the streets and check the churches at night, to be on the lookout for any stray Chinese.

These Archers of the Watch—the "Guet"—are an important feature of the Paris scene. One hundred and fifty in number, they buy their posts and then recoup their investment partly through an annual five percent return on that purchase price, and partly through receiving a major series of tax exemptions and special rebates from the city. About one-third of them are mounted on horseback; the others patrol on foot.

As one would expect, their lives are a blend of boredom, petty daily routines, ceremonial functions, and moments of major drama and danger. In recent years their lives have been made particularly hazardous by the notorious gang of robbers and cutthroats led by the young, outwardly charming wastrel known as "Cartouche." Dapperly dressed, and carrying their trademark, an elegant-looking walking stick with a metal knob—one blow from which can crush a man's skull—they have terrorized Paris for years. Though Cartouche himself was betrayed and publicly executed in 1721, along with his younger brother, members of the gang are still being rounded up by the Archers, brought to speedy trial, and executed, exiled to the galleys, or branded, often in batches of fifty or more.

The Archers also have simpler tasks, such as clearing a raceway through the streets of Paris, so that the Comte de Saillant could carry through his wild wager of riding straight to Chantilly and back twice within six hours. The King's own astronomer royal, Cassini, acted as timekeeper. By using twenty-seven different mounts, Saillant won his bet handsomely, with more than twenty minutes to spare, netting himself ten thousand francs. And that despite the fact that one of the Archers blundered into his path and almost unseated him. In their full ceremonial liveries, also, the Archers have just welcomed the ambassadors from Venice into Paris, and have also swelled the escort accompanying the young King.

The point is, they know the city well, and if anyone can

find Hu, it is they. The task should not be too hard. Hu, after all, as far as we know, is the only Chinese man in Paris.

SATURDAY, 28 NOVEMBER 1722.
PARIS

Hu is home with the Bayneses. The Archers of the Watch found him at three a.m., near the end of their night-long sweep of the city, sitting on a stone step outside the gate of the Hospital of the "Petites Maisons." That's well south of the river, on the west side of the city. Eventually they got him home, and were well tipped for their pains. It was a bitter night, and Hu was freezing cold, his clothes filthy.

It seems that, after being separated from Orry's secretary, Hu ran around the city at random, hour after hour, at some stage crossing the river and getting lost in the maze of streets on the south bank. Since he was found at the Petites Maisons, he probably took the Pont Royal and wandered down the rue du Bac until he reached the rue de Sèvres. No one knows how Hu passed the time till three a.m., but surely he saw a side of Paris he has never seen before, for the Archers' records of this period show the others they arrested in all their misery: the beggars and child prostitutes and cripples, the attempted suicides, the drunks, the window-smashers, the homeless and unemployed of almost every trade and occupation. Did Françoise Hanelin or Suzanne Galland approach Hu before making love to soldiers in the Swiss guard? Did Pierre Bajet try to sell Hu one of his fake gold rings encrusted with equally fake precious stones? Did Marguerite Orgerot shake her tin cup under his face, falsely claiming—in a language Hu still cannot understand—that the money was for the poor prisoners in jail? Most of these cold, lost souls are from Paris, but others come from distant regions of France, and some from beyond the borders, from Flanders, Piedmont, Switzerland. But no one has come as far as Hu, catechist, keeper of the gate, erstwhile copyist of Chinese texts.

Foucquet is relieved to see Hu back but does not think he is in any state to see the papal nuncio on Monday, as had been planned. Much hangs on that visit, for Monsignor Massei wishes to reassure himself by seeing Hu in person that he is ready for the journey to Rome and to be of service there. So Foucquet summarizes Hu's adventure in a letter to the nuncio's auditor, Abbé Rota, emphasizing Hu's dirtiness, carelessness, and lack of decent clothes, and asking if Hu can be excused. The nuncio says no, Hu must be brought as planned. As the Abbé Rota more delicately puts it in his reply to Foucquet: "I communicated your note to M. le Nonce, who wishes to see the Chinese on Monday in whatever state he finds himself, and he has charged me to tell you that there is no need to dress him up in better clothes, if it is his nature to ruin everything and take care of nothing."

MONDAY, 30 NOVEMBER 1722.
PARIS

Hu's audience with the papal nuncio Massei is not a success. Hu is escorted to the nuncio's residence not by Foucquet, but by that same secretary of Father Orry who had managed to lose Hu three days before at the Tuileries. The secretary passes him to Abbé Rota, who leads him to the antechamber. There Foucquet joins them.

The antechamber is filled with members of the nuncio's entourage—clerics, gentlemen, page boys. Seeing a crucifix on the wall, Hu throws himself to the floor and kowtows repeatedly, ignoring the throng of stunned onlookers, to whom Foucquet tries to explain these outward marks of a Chinese devotion. (By the missionaries' preference the kowtow is used within China only on Good Friday, the day of Christ's passion and death, though sometimes an excess of devotion carries the converts away at other times also.)

With the nuncio himself, things go no better. Led to his presence by Foucquet, Hu, before he can be greeted, sizes up the placement of the three armchairs that have been prepared for them and finds the arrangement wanting in respect for the man he takes—correctly—to be the appointed delegate of the Pope himself. Crying, *"Da zhu jiao!"*—"Reverend Bishop!"—and moving so swiftly no one has time to prevent him, Hu grasps the armchair prepared for the nuncio and pushes it to what he decides is the honorific end of the room. Seizing a second chair, he pushes it beside the first, urging Foucquet to take it. "As for me," says Hu, his task accomplished, "I will stay here." And he stands humbly at the other end of the room as Foucquet and the nuncio sit and begin their talk.

Foucquet again explains the ritual significance of Hu's actions. The nuncio, who has been in Paris only a little over one month, and had his first audience with the young King less than two weeks ago, possesses a strong sense of his own dignity, and is neither amused nor impressed by Hu's activities. The conversation is brief. Hu is permitted to take his leave, and he is returned to the Bayneses' home.

EARLY DECEMBER 1722.
PARIS

Hu dreamed the other night that his mother was dead. He is completely inconsolable. The Bayneses and Foucquet have tried to persuade him that it was just a dream, that he doesn't *know* she is dead, but Hu will not listen to them. His lamentations, his cries of sorrow, reverberate day after day.

Signs of stress are everywhere. Hu's room is filthy, and the furniture every which way, but he gets enraged with the Bayneses' daughter when she comes in to tidy up. At one stage he threatens to hit Miss Baynes unless she leaves him alone. He doesn't treat Mrs. Baynes any better, and the Bayneses have sent to ask Foucquet's advice. Foucquet has none. He feels that Hu is beyond the simple remedies that come to mind: bleeding, healthy soups, a change of diet. Mr. Baynes, forced to leave on business one day, is so nervous about what Hu might do in his absence that he locks him in his room. Hu breaks the door open, and it is Foucquet who must pay to have it repaired. On another occasion, Baynes beats Hu with his whip.

Nor will Hu help Foucquet any more with serving the Mass, that happy shared moment of devotion that they had broken off in Nantes and then, for a time, resumed. There is no church more solemn in its decorum, more handsome in its adornments, more rich in silver plate and altar hangings than the great church of the Jesuits, where the embalmed hearts of Kings Louis XIII and XIV and the great Condé are enshrined as proof-royal of the past power and patronage of the Jesuits. But now Hu shuns its opulence. Foucquet sum-

mons him to the sacristy to find an explanation. Hu obeys
the summons but will not answer Foucquet's questions. Instead, seeing, he says, a maze of crosses on the floor in the
patterns of the wooden parquet, he hops and jumps his way
to the door to avoid defiling the sacred squares.

Hu says now that the food at the Bayneses' is too good
for him; he does not need so much. He says again, as he said
at Port Louis, that he wants to beg. He wants to travel across
France, begging all the way. On occasion he has left the
Bayneses' house and accosted people for money. If kind
souls give him some coppers—and they sometimes do, for
he is a striking sight—he buys bread and stuffs his pockets
with it, and munches it walking, in the streets and public
squares.

LATE DECEMBER 1722.
PARIS

Any chance of a prompt departure for Rome by sea has
been dashed again. Foucquet has heard that the Compagnie
des Indes refused to hold the eleven crates of books in Le
Havre, so that Foucquet and Hu could join them there. Instead, all the books have been shipped up the Seine to
Rouen, by orders of the secretary of state, Dubois, and will
be brought thence to Paris and to the safekeeping of D'Argenson, of the police. Foucquet's scholarly work is perforce
at a standstill.

Foucquet and Hu do have one moment of spiritual
closeness. For the first time since he left the *Prince de Conti,*
Hu says that he would like to make his confession. Foucquet
responds with alacrity. The procedure is not without diffi-

culty, since several years before, the Archbishop of Paris, Cardinal de Noailles, urged on by the Jesuits' enemies in the universities and elsewhere in the Church, has forbidden all those attached to the Maison Professe to hear confessions within the Paris area. It is a thoroughgoing prohibition, and when the young King Louis XV wishes to make confession to his Jesuit confessor Linières, they have to go to the diocese of Chartres. Foucquet has to go to the archbishopric of Paris for a special dispensation. Cardinal de Noailles gives him permission, since it is for a Chinese.

Foucquet respects the secrecy of the confessional, and there is no record of what Hu says on that occasion. But we do know that Hu has worked out his own way of passing the time. In his room at the Bayneses' house, secretly, he constructs a drum. It is small, about six inches in diameter. He also makes a little flag, a foot across, on which he writes four Chinese characters, *"nan nü fen bie"*—"Men and women should be kept in their separate spheres." When his work is done he shows it, proudly, to Foucquet. Foucquet dismisses the objects with scorn as the amusements of a child, but does not think it right to confiscate them. He has no idea what they are for.

The next saint's day, Hu takes the flag and the drum from his room. Waving the flag aloft, beating on his drum, he marches from the Maison Professe to the neighboring parish church of St. Paul. A crowd of Parisians, drawn by the noise and by the curious sight of the marching figure, follows in his wake. In front of the great door of St. Paul's, under the strange high and contrasting triple towers that make the church so distinctive, Hu begins to preach. He preaches in Chinese, waving his banner with its simple message to emphasize his points. The crowd is large and attentive, cheering him on.

Hu starts to make a habit of going to St. Paul's with his flag and his drum. He seems to thrive on the attention, to be pleased that he is carrying his message to so many people. But after several days of this, Foucquet grows dismayed: Such crowd-pleasing actions by possible rabble-rousers are anathema to the state in the world of Jansenist religious ecstasy, and can lead to swift arrest and punishment. This is even more dangerous than begging in public places. Foucquet is negotiating at Versailles for his passport and his books, and he cannot bear the thought of any new scandals, news of which would spread swiftly over Paris since Linières has been drawing fashionable crowds to the Jesuit church with his preaching. So Foucquet arranges with Baynes to have the drum and flag taken clandestinely from Hu's room, when Hu is distracted on some other business. The flag and drum are broken up and thrown away.

Hu does not make another set. He seems too disheartened to try.

SUNDAY, 21 FEBRUARY 1723.
PARIS

Hu has disappeared again. He has been gone for a week. This is nothing like last November, when he frightened his hosts and himself by wandering for a day and a night. This time he has vanished completely, lost without a trace somewhere in the vastness of the city. The weather is vile, cold with a steady, driving rain. As far as anyone knows, Hu has no money at all. He has taken nothing with him from his room but a little bundle of personal belongings.

Foucquet hesitates to bother Police Lieutenant D'Argenson again. They have been corresponding about his books, and that has been going badly enough. The eleven crates arrived in Paris at the end of January and are in D'Argenson's hands—but secretary of state Dubois has forbidden Foucquet to take the bulk of them to Rome. It appears that the King's librarian, Bignon, intends to get his hands on them, to take Foucquet's earlier offer all too seriously, and to keep almost the entire collection for the King's library. As with most people adept at manipulating others, it has not occurred to Foucquet that all this time Bignon has been manipulating him, edging him ever nearer to pledging his library to the royal collection, answering benignly his diatribes on "Figurism" while salting away his notes for future use.

Bignon has long since lost interest in Hu, whom, in private correspondence with his friend professor Fourmont, he has said he would employ only if he "turned out not to be completely useless." Of Foucquet's theories he writes to Fourmont, "Nothing in the world has ever been so ill-founded." Accordingly, "It occurs to me that it could be useful to us to let him have free rein." When Fourmont balks a little, Bignon urges him onward: "I understand nothing of your scruples. I would not want to think that one would want to thwart our plan." These are complex games that Bignon is playing. They are equally serious for Foucquet, and for him the stakes are twenty-five years of work.

When Foucquet gets up the courage to tell D'Argenson of Hu's latest disappearance, D'Argenson once more alerts the Archers of the Watch. They have all been desperately busy for weeks, escorting the young King to the Tuileries Palace and the Louvre for the formal declaration of his majority, trying to supervise the huge crowds that turned out for the occasion—their ardor undimmed by the weather—

and trying to ensure that the fireworks displays do not lead to another fire like the one that broke out earlier in the month. But despite these distractions, D'Argenson shows how seriously he takes the charge by assigning a special officer to the search, inspector Louis Duval. If anyone can find Hu, it will be Duval. A former commander of the company of forty-three horsemen who have the task of scouring Paris on mounted patrols, Duval is now in charge of the "Garde des Ports," a special group of foot soldiers that checks out the riverside harbors and the stockpiles and warehouses in the city. All the inspectors, working under the overall direction of the lieutenant of police, have their own informants in the city, and know the hotels and boarding-houses, the brothels, the second-hand stalls and sellers of stolen goods. This is the terrain they understand.

As they hunt, the Archers and Duval find many derelicts and ne'er-do-wells in many parts of Paris. One man, pretending to be armless so as to get popular sympathy, is arrested in the church of the Petit St. Antoine; one former Archer of the Watch is now, in his turn, making a disturbance in a shop; one man, with a genuine wooden leg, has lost his job as a tailor and been reduced to begging; a thirty-nine-year-old schoolmaster from Dijon is wandering vaguely through the streets at night, apparently quite unaware where he is; and an eleven-year-old boy is brought in after knifing a horse in the thigh. The Archers even find one certified madman, Gilles Lenoir, a twenty-five-year-old from Brittany who had been shut up in a hospital once before, and released. But they can find no trace of Hu.

7

Orléans

SATURDAY, 20 FEBRUARY 1723.
JESUIT RESIDENCE, ORLÉANS

Letter from Father Léonard Gramain to Father Jean-Baptiste du Halde:

"My dear Father, the peace of the Lord be with you. Since I do not know whether or not Father Foucquet has already left for Rome, and since Father du Teil told me that he believes Father Orry is not in Paris at present, Your Reverence must forgive me for addressing him in the predicament in which we find ourselves here, one which concerns all those interested in the China Mission.

"Yesterday at seven in the evening we were amazed to find on our doorstep the Chinese whom dear Father Foucquet brought to Paris. His pitiable state aroused our compassion, and we took him in. But we have no idea what to do with him, and our predicament is all the greater because neither with words nor signs can he make us understand why he left Paris and where he wants to go. But it's clear to us that as he came here without any letter of explanation, and holding out his hands, he must have escaped while in some misfortune. Further, since he often says the words 'China' and 'Peking,' and also the words 'Rome' and 'Pope,' we are assuming that he would like to go to Rome and from there to China.

"If dear Father Foucquet is in Paris, please be so good as to ask him to let me know as soon as possible what he wants done. Have him write to me as he did once before, in Chinese but using our alphabet, with an accompanying translation into French, telling me what to say to this poor unfortunate man.

"If Father Foucquet has already left, give me your instructions—or to me jointly with Father Orry—without further delay. If I can I will look after this unhappy man until I get your instructions. But I'm afraid he may run away from us too, unless all he suffered in coming here may serve to discourage him from making another such journey.

"I am counting on a prompt reply. While awaiting it I have the honor to be, Reverend Father, your most humble
Gramain."

WEDNESDAY, 24 FEBRUARY 1723.
ORLÉANS

Hu wants to return to Paris at once. He had actually packed up his bundle of possessions when the director of the household affairs at the residence, Father Viane, found him and led him back to his room. Hu has been made to unpack, and urged—with signs—to be patient. But it is a tricky business: there is nowhere in the residence to lock Hu up should he really try to flee.

A letter from Foucquet, in Chinese and French as requested by Gramain, has agitated Hu still further. In this letter, which Gramain reads aloud, sounding out the unfamiliar words, Foucquet says that he will be leaving soon for Rome. Obviously Hu is terrified that Foucquet plans to leave without him.

Foucquet has told the police lieutenant D'Argenson that Hu is in Orléans, and the Paris search for him has been called off. But Foucquet has left no precise instructions about what is to be done. He is trying to find alternative housing for Hu. He feels the Bayneses have gone through enough, although they have loyally offered to take Hu back again.

THURSDAY, 25 FEBRUARY 1723.
ORLÉANS

They have stopped having to use sign language and gestures in the Orléans Jesuit residence when they try to communicate with Hu. By an astounding coincidence—it may well be Divine Providence—they have found an interpreter. He is a prosperous grocer in the city, formerly from Blois, now living in Orléans, who served as the chief cook on the embassy of Cardinal Maillard de Tournon to Emperor Kangxi that left for China in 1705. He lived almost three years in China and Macao, and speaks the language fluently. Hu is astonished when he hears this Frenchman speak. "You must be from my land," says Hu.

Now that he can speak Chinese again, Hu unloads his grievances. He has been four years in Foucquet's service, he says, and has never been paid a penny. He should be getting ten taels a year. He came to Europe, he says, so that he could go as quickly as possible to Paris and Rome, and then home

again to China. One can see that Hu's saying he has served
Foucquet for four years—when in fact they have only been
together fourteen months—has a kind of logic to it. For if
Hu has convinced himself that he has served for four years,
and the fact that the contract with Foucquet was for five
years in all is engraved on his mind, then Hu only has one
year left to serve, and he can begin his mental plans for
returning to China from Rome. Perhaps, too, some innate
caution makes him say he was promised ten taels a year,
when in fact the contract stipulated twenty. You should not
press your case too hard with the enemy.

Foucquet has still given no firm instructions about what
he personally intends to do with Hu. Not knowing yet that
Father Gramain has found an interpreter in Orléans—how
would he ever have guessed that?—Foucquet sends another
of his letters written out both in a phonetic spelling of the
Chinese and in French, which Gramain again reads aloud.
The letter is full of complaints about Hu's behavior, and de-
clares that Foucquet will have no more to do with Hu unless
Hu behaves himself better. Jumping at Father Gramain, Hu
seizes the letter out of the startled man's hands. Before anyone can prevent him, he tears the letter to angry pieces. For
this act of insolence, he is roundly cuffed by Gramain's servant. The letter is gone for good.

MONDAY, 8 MARCH 1723.
ORLÉANS

Letter from Gramain to Foucquet:

"Up to now I have been doing everything I can to make
our Chinese wait here patiently, but I don't think I am going

to be able to make him stay here much longer, however much I wish to do what will please you. For seven or eight days he has been plunged into a melancholy that makes me fear for the consequences. Yesterday morning he packed up his bundle and was already outside the residence, on the point of leaving, when one of our fathers ran after him and brought him back.

"I at once sent for our interpreter, who happened to be out in the countryside and only returned at night. But this morning at eight o'clock he came to see me and I had him speak to your Chinese. As far as I can understand it, what Hu wants at any price is to rejoin you in Paris. With great difficulty I have persuaded him to stay here five or six days more, and I only got to that point by promising him that I would write to you asking, as I am now doing, that you take him back. And I told him that if, after the five or six days that I asked of him, I had received no instructions from you, I would let him go. And, no doubt about it, I will have to. . . .

"Give me your instructions, with all the confidence of a friend. I will try to prove to you that you have not acted wrongly in trusting me.

Gramain."

FRIDAY, 12 MARCH 1723.
ORLÉANS

Hu has again been going regularly to the splendid church attached to the Jesuit residence in Orléans, where among the other objects of devotion hangs the painting with its representation of the four quarters of the earth, and the Lord above in His glory. Sometimes Hu worships meekly, head uncovered, hands at his sides. Sometimes he insists on wearing his hat even in the church, claiming that in China that is how one shows respect for the Emperor.

One night, in the garden of the residence, a teacher in the college sees Hu standing under the full moon, his arms outstretched.

Foucquet has been sending a stream of letters to Father Gramain, which he askes Gramain to pass on to Hu via the interpreter. These letters urge Hu to recognize that he did wrong when he fled Paris for no shadow of a reason. The latest letter suggests that Hu should write a formal letter of contrition to Foucquet, requesting pardon for his fault.

Through the interpreter, Gramain relays this request to Hu. Hu says that he will never write such a letter, that he has committed no fault. He would rather have his hands cut off, he cries, than write such a letter to Foucquet.

TUESDAY, 16 MARCH 1723.
ORLÉANS

Hu has left Orléans. He was put aboard the coach that left for Paris at 2 a.m. His ticket cost six francs, and Gramain gave the coachman another two francs and a few sous so that he would see to Hu's food en route and deliver him safely to the Maison Professe in Paris, where Foucquet has secured him lodging.

Despite his protestations of eagerness to return to Paris, and his delight when the instructions finally came from Foucquet, Hu made difficulties when he heard he was leaving at 2 a.m. He said that he did not want to leave at night but only by daylight, that he did not want to go by coach but on foot, with money given to him for food.

The gentle Father Gramain became angry. He told Hu

he had made the reservation and bought the tickets and that was that. If Hu didn't take the coach he would be thrown out of his bed anyway, and turned out of the Jesuit residence. Hu then changed his tune, and after a farewell meal, was escorted by the interpreter and Gramain's valet to the inn near the stagecoach stop, to get a bit of sleep before it departed.

Before leaving the residence Hu did thank Gramain graciously, through the interpreter, for all his kindnesses. And Gramain sent a bill to Foucquet for sixteen francs and five sous' travel expenses, to cover the costs of Hu's two journeys from Orléans, both this current one and the one he had made the previous November. Gramain said the Orléans Fathers would take care of all the other expenses for food and lodging incurred while Hu was staying with them. Nobody, of course, had to pay any expenses for Hu's journey *from* Paris *to* Orléans. Hu had taken care of that himself.

8

The Road to Charenton

SUNDAY, 28 MARCH 1723.
PARIS

Hu is living in the church of St. Louis, the Jesuit church attached to the Maison Professe. He has a little corner room off one of the galleries that circle, at two different levels, the soaring nave. By day, the light flows into the church through the windows in the spacious dome, making a shimmering richness out of the marble sculptures and wooden carvings, and the four massive paintings that tell stories from the reign of the church's patron saint. By night the elaborately posed men and angels writhe in the cool darkness. Hu's room has in it a bed, a wicker chair, and a table. One window, which Hu keeps always open, gives onto the world outside. It is infinitely less spacious or comfortable than the apartment at the Baynes house, but Hu expresses himself well satisfied.

It is the superior of the Maison Professe, the eighty-one-year-old Father Gaillard, who has given Foucquet permission to lodge Hu here, but only for a few weeks, until Hu and Foucquet leave for Rome.

Foucquet is writing yet again to the King's librarian, Bignon, but now he is less anxious and less effusive than he was in the past. Some of his books have already been yielded up by D'Argenson to the papal nuncio, who is arranging for them to be shipped to Rome. The others will surely follow soon. Full of confidence, not only does Foucquet refuse to accept any arguments that by helping to clear the books through customs Bignon set up a prior claim to the contents of the crates, but he boldly asks Bignon to lend him some of the books that were in the seven crates that he and Bretesche bought for the library—he especially wants the twenty-volume set of works on Ming Dynasty ritual. He would like to work on the texts while in Rome.

Hu is out in the streets again. He has been wandering at will, leaving each morning with the expense money he is given daily for his food. He buys whatever suits his fancy whenever he is hungry, and eats it wherever he happens to be. He postures, he clowns, he chants. He is becoming quite well known in the Marais, perhaps even farther afield. It is as if he has entered the carnival world that Paris becomes once the great spring fairs reopen and all the rules relax. It is a world of wildness and freedom, where freaks, exotics, topsy-turvy beings are accepted by the crowds, clustered around, cheered on their way with shouts and laughter.

Hu seems content. He has not made any drawings since Port Louis, he talks no more of writing up his travels. He refuses, absolutely, Foucquet's final request that he settle down and begin to copy Chinese texts. Foucquet says he will never pay him if he does not work. Hu shrugs. When Foucquet brandishes the work contract at him, the one made in Canton, Hu tries to grab it out of his hands.

THURSDAY, 8 APRIL 1723.
PARIS

Everything has come together. The passport for travel to Rome has been issued by the secretary of state, Dubois. The papal nuncio is all encouragement. Police lieutenant D'Argenson is courteous over the remaining books. And Bignon seems reconciled. The first batch of Foucquet's books has been handed over to the nuncio and already shipped to Marseilles for passage by sea to Rome. The Jesuit superiors' opposition to the Roman journey seems to have faded away. The only problem could be that Father Gaillard, hearing one too many stories of Hu's antics in the streets, has ordered him out of his little room in the church and forbidden him further residence in the Maison Professe. But Foucquet pleads, successfully, for just two or three days' more grace, for then they will be gone.

Foucquet makes reservations for two on the stagecoach leaving for Lyons on 12 April, and pays the advance. He hurries to find Hu and gives him the news.

SATURDAY, 10 APRIL 1723.
PARIS

Hu won't go.

That's what he told Foucquet on Thursday, and that's what he still says. Foucquet at first tries banter: "The Pope has summoned me," he says to Hu. "He's calling you as well." He tries self-interest: "You'll lack for nothing in

Rome. People will do everything they can to make you happy." He tries vague threats: "If you don't want to come with me, when I have left Paris, who will take care of you?" Hu knits his brows and says no word.

Foucquet sends a messenger to tell the papal nuncio of this new development. The nuncio sends his intendant, Marc Cardinali, to visit Hu. Foucquet acts as interpreter. Cardinali finds Hu unshakable in his determination not to go to Rome.

Apart from a quick morning trip outside the church to buy some bread, Hu stays in his little room. Someone has told him, or he has understood them to say, that Foucquet kills people. Hu seems to think that the message comes from the Jesuit superior, Father Gaillard, though heaven knows how he got that idea. He also seems to think that in some way he is involved in Foucquet's alleged guilt. Hu is in great fear. He lies in the bed, the window open, but makes no pretense of being ill. Doubtless he would lock the door, but the room has no key. If Foucquet or anyone comes to remonstrate with him, he pulls the covers over his head.

SUNDAY, 11 APRIL 1723.
PARIS

It is after dinner. People are crowded inside and around the doorway of Hu's cubicle in the church. There is Foucquet. There is Baynes, who has been summoned as a man with experience in handling Hu. There is the papal nuncio's intendant, Marc Cardinali. There are two Jesuits from the Maison Professe, who have orders from the superior, Father Gaillard, to throw Hu out. And there are others drawn by curiosity. At first Foucquet tries to reason with Hu, but soon he raises his voice in anger. Hu shouts back, matching threat for threat.

It is getting dark. The coach booking is for 4 a.m. the following morning. They decide to take Hu to an inn near the Hôtel de Sens, from which the coach will be leaving, on the large stretch of open land that lies along the river opposite the Pont Marie. They can then see how Hu behaves in the early morning.

Hu refuses to leave his room. Three strong servants are brought from the Maison Professe. They carry Hu, struggling and striking out with his fists, down the narrow stairs, and as he struggles still, crying out in rage and fear, they carry him along the darkened streets toward the inn. It is not a long walk at all, just a hundred paces or so down from the Maison Professe. A room is rented for the night at the Inn of St. Catherine, and Hu is locked inside. Foucquet arranges for supper to be sent up to him.

Foucquet goes back to his own room at the Maison Professe, which tomorrow he will be leaving forever, and takes up his pen. He addresses a letter to the lieutenant of police, D'Argenson:

"Sir,

"In the difficult situation where Providence has placed me, I make so bold yet again to beg for your authority and your assistance, as I have done on other occasions. I am humbly and deeply grateful for the help you gave me then.

"I leave tomorrow for Rome, by the Lyons coach. For many reasons I am no longer free to put off this journey. I had counted on taking with me that same Chinese on whose account I have already taken the liberty of writing to you. This man has fallen into a state of mental imbalance which is not to be believed. He now no longer wishes to come to Rome with me, even though he yearned a thousand times to see that famous city, and when we first sailed he said that was his reason for making the journey. But that is only part of it. He wishes, he says, to return to China by land, and to make the journey on foot. He began such a journey last time, when he reached Orléans, in the worst possible weather and without a penny of travel money. I made sure that he was brought back by public coach.

"Since his return to Paris his follies have grown ever greater. He told me on first coming here that an angel had appeared before him, and had urged him on to great deeds—on which he did not elaborate. He has said the same thing at other times since then. I will not give a list here of all his other absurdities, but in sum at certain times—no longer rare—he ceases to be reasonable. His acts of folly are accompanied by a malevolence and an obstinacy that can not be relieved by prayers, threats, or generosity.

"Finding myself in a situation where I cannot force him to come, and must therefore leave him behind, I believe, Sir, that I should inform you of his true nature. It is clear that this unfortunate man will fall into a miserable state if he is not restrained and sent to a place where they keep people like him. He will roam all Paris begging, perhaps the whole kingdom, creating scenes that it would be preferable to avoid.

"My desire and hope to see him change his ways made me put off sharing this knowledge with you until this mo-ment. I beg you to take note of what I say, and to order the arrest of this wretched man. Perhaps he will come back to

himself, once he is arrested and has no liberty to do everything he chooses. I will have a special obligation to you, and
taking once more my leave I have the honor to assure you
that I am, most respectfully,

Sir,

Yours etc.

Foucquet

Paris 11 April 1723"

Foucquet goes back to his packing. He still has a large
number of clothes that have to be sorted through, not to
mention all the books that he has acquired since he arrived
in Paris. When combined with those in the eleven crates,
they will give him a truly superb research collection.

MONDAY, 12 APRIL 1723.
PARIS

Though it is not yet four o'clock in the morning, a little
group has assembled to see off Father Foucquet. Baynes is
there, yet again, and another Englishman called Smith, also
a Catholic, who was a mathematics student of Foucquet's at
the college of La Flèche twenty-six years before. Smith has
brought along his son. Marc Cardinali, who promised to be
there, has not yet arrived.

Foucquet goes to Hu's room, to try to reason with him
one more time, and persuade him to make the coach journey
to Rome. Hu is still in a rage and will not listen. It is clear
he cannot be made to go.

The coach is waiting. Foucquet's luggage is aboard. If
Hu had agreed to come, Foucquet would have been able to

throw away his letter to police lieutenant D'Argenson. Now he decides to deliver it. Since Cardinali, the logical person for such an errand, has still not arrived, he hands the letter to Baynes. Foucquet has with him one thousand francs, money given him by the papal nuncio to meet all the expenses of the journey to Rome. On impulse, he takes one hundred francs and gives them to Baynes, telling him to use the money in looking after Hu. Right there, in the street by the side of the waiting coach, the Englishman Baynes scrawls out a hurried receipt in slightly inaccurate French.

Foucquet climbs aboard, the doors are latched shut; there are calls to the horses and the cracking of whips, and the big public coach rumbles off on its way to Lyons, where connecting coaches can be had for Strasbourg or Rome.

Somewhere in the coach—probably in the cheapest section inside at the back, away from the doors and the windows—there is an empty seat.

THURSDAY, 15 APRIL 1723.
PARIS

Baynes and Cardinali have come to collect Hu. Baynes has a rented carriage, and Cardinali is on horseback. Baynes has brought a friend along in case the going gets rough.

Hu has been shut in his room at St. Catherine's Inn for more than four days, some of the time tied up with rope, ever since late Sunday night. It took a great deal of persuasion, two personal visits, and more money than they expected for Baynes and Cardinali to induce the innkeeper to feed and house Hu for so long. Hu has made no attempt to escape.

It has taken four days to get the papers that are needed to have Hu committed to an insane asylum, which Foucquet and the papal nuncio both decided was the only solution if Hu refused to go to Rome. If Hu ever gets better, he can be sent back to China on some ship of the Compagnie des Indes.

Marc Cardinali met up with Baynes at 5 a.m. on the Monday morning, just after Foucquet's departure. He was flustered and chagrined to have arrived too late for the send-off. His valet had fallen sound asleep and forgotten to wake him. By eight, Baynes and Cardinali were at police lieutenant D'Argenson's office, to hand-deliver Foucquet's letter and seek official help. But by bad luck, D'Argenson was at the Palace of Versailles for one of his regular meetings with the young King and Cardinal Dubois, secretary of state. D'Argenson's staff told Baynes and Cardinali to come back on Wednesday.

Nobody wanted to wait so long. The papal nuncio, Massei, dispatched his own assistant, the auditor Rota, to Versailles on Tuesday. Rota, conferring with secretary of state Dubois, secured a *lettre de cachet* to have Hu committed to the asylum at Charenton. Such letters—under the authority of which individuals can be put away for years without formal trial of any kind—are issued in the King's name by the secretary of state and passed on to the lieutenant of police for implementation. Probably Dubois passed the letter over to D'Argenson while the lieutenant was still at Versailles, though he may have had it delivered to the police office in Paris. Baynes and Cardinali kept their appointment with D'Argenson on Wednesday night, for now they could speed him up on the matter of the *lettre de cachet*. D'Argenson promised to see to the final details, telling them to return at

11 a.m. on Thursday. They did so. D'Argenson handed over a copy of the secretary of state's commitment order and a covering letter to the superior of the Brothers of Charity, who manage the Charenton asylum. He told them the King's exchequer would see to the payment of all expenses.

Arriving at St. Catherine's Inn, Baynes and Cardinali pay off the innkeeper and go to Hu's room. Both are carrying their whips. Since neither of them has any way of explaining their intentions to Hu, all they can do is hustle him bodily out of his room and into the street. Something—the waiting coach, the bright light, the expressions on their faces—terrifies Hu. He slashes out with his fingers at Cardinali's face. Cardinali jumps back, but Hu catches his shirt and rips it right down the front. Baynes is hitting at Hu with his whip, Cardinali does the same, and with the help of Baynes's friend they drag Hu toward the carriage. Hu throws himself down to the ground, to prevent them taking him further, and a curious crowd of Parisians begins to gather. Though these idlers have no idea what is happening, they seem to feel sympathy for Hu. Cardinali forces back the onlookers while Baynes and his friend drag Hu into their carriage and throw themselves inside with him. They pull a pair of manacles over Hu's wrists and lock them shut.

The carriage moves off. Cardinali mounts his horse and rides along beside them as escort. There are two fast routes from St. Catherine's Inn to the Porte St. Antoine, where the Charenton road begins: one leads past the Maison Professe and the mighty domed Jesuit church of St. Louis; one past the strange triple towers of the parish church of St. Paul. A face pressed to the carriage window, chin resting on manacled hands, would be bound to see one or the other as it was hurtled by.

9

Inside Charenton

There are four main buildings containing cells for the insane in the hospital of Charenton. They all meet at a central point, in the form of an asymmetrical cross. Each building is three stories high, with an added attic floor under mansard roofs. Each building is constructed in the same pattern, with two rows of cells on each floor, leading off a central corridor.

Abutting the right-hand end of this complex is the refectory building for the Brothers of Charity. Above the refectory room is a large spacious salon, used to entertain important visitors and to hold certain formal convocations. On the top floor, over the salon, is a chapel for the patients, which they can reach by a separate internal staircase. From their refectory the Brothers of Charity can walk along a corridor above the kitchen block that leads to a little bridge. This bridge passes over another small internal courtyard and takes you into the twenty acres of spacious gardens and the home farm that are one of the glories of Charenton. Here are not only elegant walkways under avenues of walnut trees, but also the vegetable gardens and vineyards that supply much of the hospital's needs. Across the fields and gardens are spacious views to the parkland and royal château of Vincennes. At the far end of the gardens, to the west, is the hospital's own cemetery. The gardens are not made available to most of the patients, as the surrounding walls are too low for security.

The gardens lie on a ridge of land about sixty feet high that runs across the country here, parallel to the river Marne. That same ridge falls steeply down toward the river at the point where the dormitories for the mad patients have been built, and to hold back the soil from slippage the face of the slope has been shored up with blocks of cut stone that rise up several yards higher than the roofs of the buildings. The rear ends of one of the dormitory buildings and the refectory are backed at right angles into this great retaining wall and joined at their other end to the dormitory wings that run from east to west, parallel to the river Marne. Thus, with the simple addition of only one length of high wall, two exitless courtyards have been created.

These courtyards get no sun, since they are not very wide and the buildings are high. The courtyards are also cut off from the winds from all four directions, and for this reason the smell there from the hospital and the dormitories' own human waste is extremely strong. The Brothers of Charity have discussed the matter at the full meetings of their little group—there are ten Brothers in all, and they talk over hospital matters quite often, casting secret ballots on major decisions using black and white stones—but they are not quite sure what to do about it. They have thought of moving some of the key services, such as the dispensary, and perhaps some of their own lodgings, farther away from the smell. They have also thought of constructing some more efficient latrines.

Hu lies on his mattress in the courtyard. He has been brought outside on the orders of the prior of the hospital, because he has rarely left his bed since Baynes and Cardinali delivered him to Charenton on 15 April; the prior believes that a little air—even this air—will do him good. If Hu looks upward, he can see the sky.

TUESDAY, 27 JULY 1723.
ROME

Foucquet had a fairly uneventful trip to Rome, though he was ill for some of the time. On the way to Lyons he visited his older married sister at her husband's estate in Avallon, between the rivers Yonne and Serein. Leaving Lyons, he crossed the Alps and passed through Turin and Milan, reaching Rome on June 4.

Foucquet was received in audience by the Pope, Innocent XIII, almost right away, on 8 June. They talked for two hours on China and the rites. It was extremely gratifying, all the more so in light of the fact that His Holiness had recently been seriously ill.

Foucquet is not staying with the Jesuits, despite the wealth and size of their establishment in Rome. Instead, he has been invited to live, on the orders of the Pope himself, in a spacious apartment in the college building of the Sacred Congregation. As well as the Pope, he has met both the prefect and the secretary of the Sacred Congregation, Cardinal

Sacripante and Monsignor Caraffa. Because they supervise all mission work, these men are the ultimate superiors of Father Perroni, the original hirer—in Canton, half a world away—of Hu.

Foucquet has not entirely forgotten Hu, and the letters he has received from Baynes and Cardinali have not reassured him that Hu is being looked after properly. At the time he committed Hu with the *lettre de cachet,* Baynes assured the prior of Charenton that the King—via D'Argenson or Dubois—would pay Hu's expenses, but apparently the money was never delivered. Cardinali has written to report the same prior as saying that he will not keep Hu unless some money is paid in promptly, and none has yet been forthcoming. The unexpected contacts with Sacripante and Caraffa seem providential to Foucquet, for he now has direct access through them to the cardinals who compose the special committee formed by the Pope to consider the problems of the China Mission. Surely Hu can be considered a China problem. Foucquet begins to draft an appeal to the cardinals on behalf of "a Chinese man-of-letters named John Hu"—Foucquet now uses the Italian form, "Giovanni Hu."

Foucquet does not personally write to Hu, since he has an enormous amount to do. He has to prepare all his ideas on the Chinese rites, and on the question of whether or not they are superstitious in nature, for scrutiny by the most learned churchmen. He has to prepare a meticulous account of his relations with the other Jesuits in China and the contacts that all of them had—or did not have—with the papal legate Mezzabarba back in the spring of 1721, and present his version of events to a special investigative commission of cardinals. He has to organize his own ideas on the interpretation of the earliest ideographs and texts in China, and their covert code that shows in them the traces of the one true religion. And there are still problems with his own books. There was a final attempt, possibly instigated by Bignon, to have all the ones he'd left in Paris confiscated, but the papal nuncio Massei is keeping up the pressure on Cardinal Dubois, and there are hopes they will soon be dispatched to Rome. So Foucquet will have most of his library in one place again, though there are still twelve hundred volumes in Peking, not counting those he left behind in Canton.

Foucquet is also involved in a correspondence of growing bitterness and anger with the French King's confessor, Father Linières. Linières has been cordial enough over Foucquet's problems with his Chinese books, but now he finds Foucquet strident in his views, rash in his behavior, and over-critical of the former Jesuit colleagues with whom he is arguing about the rites. "It seems to me," he writes to Foucquet on 29 June, "that you might have done better to have learned a bit less Chinese, and to have spent the time instead studying the sciences of saintliness."

"That letter is little worthy of you," Foucquet responds. He must say with all frankness that the Jesuits owe ultimate obedience and loyalty to the Pope, and not to one another. At all important moments in the past—including leaving Peking at almost no notice, ruining a period of study, losing many of his books, and embarking at fifty-seven on stormy seas—he has followed the path of obedience. The confessor's criticisms are out of place. Foucquet ends with a flourish and a jab, as he likes to do in his letters: "I hope that this letter will give you pleasure. Nothing would prove to me better that you do indeed love sincerity and candor, as you are always saying."

In any case, by a stroke of luck Foucquet has found another Chinese in Rome, a well-educated and courteous young man, sent to study there for the priesthood, who is more than happy to help Foucquet translate his Chinese texts. So Hu turns out not to have been really necessary after all.

THURSDAY, 21 OCTOBER 1723.
CHARENTON

Foucquet is right to be nervous over the money question, and the problems Hu will face if cash is not made available to the Brothers of Charity at Charenton. It is not that the Brothers are greedy people—far from it, they spend their whole lives caring for the old, the ill, and the seriously disturbed. But it has become a sort of expectation in the order of St. John of God that the Charenton operation will turn a profit. That surplus in turn is fed back to the central office of the order, which levies what is for all intents and purposes a "tax" on Charenton of three thousand francs a year. Or else it is passed on—after votes on the merits of each case by the Brothers of Charenton meeting jointly—in the form of gifts or grants to the poorer houses of the order, which might be in debt or even threatened with having to close a convalescent home. Such gifts are often to the tune of hundreds of francs, rising at times to block grants of a thousand francs or more, along with furniture and silverware unexpectedly presented to Charenton (or left to the Brothers by deceased patients).

The hospital at Charenton also has a host of other problems that are distracting to the Brothers of Charity and expensive to handle. The refectory roof leaks, and a major rebuilding project had to be shelved because rising costs of day labor and building materials led the contractor to threaten canceling his agreement. The reservoir they rely on for their water has also got leaks, and the wheels of the heavy pumps powered by horses are cracked and rotted in places, leading to a high risk of accidents. Money flows out, too, in land deals to guarantee their future solvency, such as buying extra farmland in the hills above Charenton, or purchasing houses in Charenton village that can be redesigned as shops and rented out to tradesmen, their attics being let as furnished rooms. Sometimes expansion is paid for by straightforward deals—selling the five small houses in the Faubourg St. Antoine at the Paris end of the Charenton road, for instance, to buy two nice ones—at ten thousand francs and eight thousand, five hundred—in Charenton itself. There are vines to root up or replant, shade trees needed for the avenues and coppice, manure for all the farmland to be bought in bulk from nearby stables.

The Brothers of Charity have a most favorable agreement with the parish of Charenton, to whom they pay only a tiny ground rent of thirty sous the acre for their large expanse of garden. But to set off against that, there are the ceaseless fights over land and rights with the lord of Charenton, Laurière, and his wife, who is as bad as he is. The couple block off access to land in front of the hospital with stone walls, "throwing a tourniquet around them all," as the recorder Brother phrased it, and for a time preventing any supplies reaching them by boat along the Marne. Costly lawyers have to be hired on such occasions, though the Brothers can call on their own supporters: Carré Le Jeune serves as their procurer in the Paris Parlement, and the Robillards of Orléans (the son is a lawyer in the parlement there, his father an inmate of Charenton) are willing to make hefty loans on advantageous terms.

Charenton makes no money from pauper patients like Hu. It draws its income from its fame as a hospital for the senile or the mad, and when such people pay, they are looked after handsomely enough. Indeed, the regulations require the prior to visit each of these "pensioners," as they are called, twice in every week—"as much to console them as to have good knowledge of their situation"—and thus furnish accurate reports to their relatives at home. With a log fire in winter, a southern exposure with views of the river, tapestries on the wall, and coverings on the floor, even the buildings where Hu is living can be made quite comfortable. And there is, in addition, beyond the Brothers' refectory and the kitchens, a separate hospital building for the dangerously ill, one massive room with fourteen beds in two neat rows and an altar at the north end, so services can be conducted there without the sick leaving their beds.

This was the original heart of the endowment, given by Sébastien Leblanc, controller-general of the army, in 1641 to the Brothers of Charity of the religious order of St. John of God. The hospital itself is kept as clean as possible, for many of the Brothers of Charity sleep in a row of rooms one floor above the main ward. Some of the wealthy pensioners—whose faculties are still quite sound—can live in one of the dormitories with the other Brothers, east of the main hospital, near the conservatory and the beautiful formal garden of the prior's residence. There is a room there for billiards, and some of the most favored pensioners are even allowed to stroll in the great garden on the hill, that same garden where the walls are too low to let the dangerous inmates roam.

For a lifetime commitment as a pensioner of the hospital, the Brothers of Charity ask for six thousand francs. Since many families do not have such a huge sum in cash, payment is accepted in lands or houses, sometimes in notes of exchange on the new banks that are flourishing—and sometimes crashing, so one must be careful—in France at this time. Some families even commit an insane relative to a lifetime at Charenton on the promise of the inheritance they will receive when that relative dies, as the former King's Musketeer Jean Batiste Sainfray did in the case of his lunatic elder brother, Pierre. This is an actuarial gamble for the Brothers of Charity: the aged François Robillard, for instance, has been there thirteen years, and more than out-eaten his welcome. Over and above these lump sum payments, the families pay—during the life of their committed relatives—a further sum of between one hundred twenty and one hundred fifty francs a year for food and extra clothing.

Most of the pensioners at Charenton are accepted on a fee-paying basis. There are two basic annual rates, one starting at nine hundred francs and rising to twelve hundred, the other ranging from twelve hundred to two thousand francs. Those paying the higher fees receive some chicken or other poultry with every main meal. The amount of meat goes down correspondingly as the fees fall.

Some of these pensioners are very rich, and their personal possessions far exceed in value most people's entire annual income. When Baron Leveneur gave his embroidered coat and waistcoat to the Brothers to sell so that they could buy a new covering for the altar in the pensioners' little chapel, they realized five hundred francs from the sale of those two garments alone. There is even an English aristocrat of sorts in residence, a Mr. Manners, an illegitimate elder brother of the previous Duke of Rutland. He has been in Charenton eight or nine years already. Perhaps, like Baynes, he originally came to France in the service of the exiled King James, and stayed till age caught him. Perhaps the scandals around his birth were so dramatic that his English relatives wanted him as far away as possible.

No money at all has been coming in to Charenton for Hu, though at the time he was first committed there seemed three probable sources of income: Baynes, the French state, and the Catholic Church. Baynes has spent forty of the hundred francs that Foucquet left him on settling Hu's hotel bill at the Inn of St. Catherine, and on the various expenses for coach rental to transport Hu to Charenton and check on him later, but he has been sitting on the remaining sixty. Neither secretary of state Dubois nor police lieutenant D'Argenson has followed up on their promise that the King would defray the costs until Hu was well enough to be released. And though the cardinals meeting in Rome did, on Foucquet's urging, vote to grant a sum of money through the papal nuncio in Paris either to pay for Hu's return to China if he came back to his senses or to keep him in Charenton if he continued to act in a deranged fashion, the money has never been sent. The trouble was that the cardinals phrased their offer with extreme caution, telling the nuncio to pay for Hu with funds from the Sacred Congregation only if the Brothers of Charity refused to pay for his basic food and lodging themselves. The nuncio, interpreting this as a request for him to seek "the greatest advantage for the Sacred Congregation" as well as "that which is most suitable for the Chinese himself," had a meeting with the prior of Charenton in October, and persuaded him to keep Hu on as a charity case.

There is no evidence that the Brothers of Charity ever deliberately mistreat Hu, though certainly the records of their behavior show a certain dandified languor in addition to their daily rounds of dedicated work among the sick. Some play their billiards for high stakes, some walk out in the countryside alone or even in disguise, some hover in the kitchens warming themselves by the cooking fires. There are those who flaunt watches or expensive snuffboxes, who have a soft cloth collar peeping out at the neck, false cuffs on their sleeves, fine stockings, a warm body-fitting *justau-corps* pulled over their robes, even brass buckles on their sensible shoes. Some wear their hair too long, some use the diminutive form of address to the pensioners and patients. Somebody has been discharging firearms in the hospital grounds, presumably one of the Brothers of Charity doing a little hunting, for surely none of the pensioners has a gun. In fact, it is unlikely that many of the Brothers of Charity see Hu very often. The poor patients are left in the hands of a layman, the almoner Lecomte, who works on a contractual basis. The Brothers do not have much faith in Lecomte, but it is not easy to find a replacement for such a job.

The greatest problem with being a charity patient in Charenton, and the cause of the "humiliation and suffering" such patients feel, in the words of those who know them, may just be the accumulation of undramatic things: the loneliness and the cold, the lack of the little luxuries that the richer patients enjoy, of access to the dispensary and bath house or to space where one can stretch and roam, the absence of sunlight, the absence of candles, of books to read or anything to do, the absence of what Baynes—in a fit of generosity that he never follows through on—calls "some little thing to amuse him or to lighten his spirit" that he would take to Hu. No shoes are issued to the poorest patients; they get no clean linen and no fresh bedclothes. Hu came to Charenton with his Vannes suit, already seriously worn, and two sets of Chinese clothes. As these wear out, they will not be replaced.

The prior does not know much about these mundane details, but he is worried about Hu's spiritual condition. When asked—by signs, by gestures—if he wants to make confession or receive the sacraments, Hu signals "No."

FRIDAY, 22 OCTOBER 1723 —
THURSDAY, 9 AUGUST 1725.
CHARENTON

Nobody really knows if Hu is mad or sane; some say one thing, some another. The papal nuncio's auditor, Abbé Rota, thinks for a while that Hu "has come back to his senses." Cardinali finds Hu "more or less enraged." Baynes doesn't inquire any more. He's used up all Foucquet's money on his trips to Charenton. The papal nuncio, as nuncios should, reserves judgment on the whole but thinks it best not to send Hu home at the moment. D'Argenson has forbidden anyone to visit Hu at Charenton without express permission from his office, so Hu has no other visitors. The prior makes a desultory attempt to find someone who speaks Chinese, so that Hu might tell them what he himself thinks about it all, but there doesn't seem to be anyone around and the search ceases.

Though there is no absolute uniformity in the size of the cells where the pauper inmates of Charenton live, they are all about twelve feet deep, from seven to nine feet across. The interior walls are twenty inches thick. The doors are made of two-inch oak planks, and open inwards. They are fastened from the outside with both a lock and a bolt. At the height of about three feet from the ground, each door has a squared-off opening, with a shutter that can be bolted on the outside. Food and drink can be conveniently passed through the opening to the patients within, when the Brothers of Charity who run the hospital think it more sensible not to enter themselves.

The walls and the ceilings of the cells are coated with plaster. The floors on the upper stories are brick; those on the ground floor are paved in coarse stone. At the end of each cell, directly opposite the door, there is one window, about three feet wide and four and a half feet high. The panes are glazed—though the glass is often broken or missing—and the windows slide along wooden runners so that they can be raised or lowered by the patients themselves. Outside the window frames iron bars, crisscrossing several times, prevent any escape.

Some of the cells on the upper floors have fireplaces, and the rooms on the southern face have a view across the broad entrance courtyard—which is sometimes used by the local villagers as a sort of public park—and down across gently sloping land to the banks of the River Marne. At the water's edge there is a little dock, where river barges unload supplies needed by the hospital. The windows of all the cells on the ground floors can be closed from the outside, beyond the bars, with wooden shutters. Those cells are then in total darkness.

In every cell, the beds are fixed in place in a corner by the window; they consist of a frame made from heavy beams, each two to three inches square, braced against the wall along two sides supported by a leg of the same thick timber on the outward corner. Smaller planks are slotted across these beams to make the surface of the bed, and a mattress is laid on the planks.

In every cell, set against the wall near the door to the corridor, there is what looks like a solid wooden box with a large oval hole cut in its top. Inside the box, underneath the hole, there is a bucket for human waste. Cut through the wall to the corridor, at ground level, there is a square opening that is sealed off by a hatch of oak, bolted on the outside. When the bucket is full, the hatch can be opened from outside and the bucket taken out into the corridor and emptied, again without anyone having to enter the cell.

For the entire period of time between 21 October 1723—when the prior and nuncio agree to continue keeping Hu shut in Charenton as a charity patient—until 9 August 1725, a period of 658 days, only one single item of precise information on John Hu is known. One of the staff at Charenton gives him a warm blanket, of good quality, to ward away the night cold. Hu tears the blanket to shreds.

10

Release

Someone is speaking Chinese to Hu. He has not heard his native language spoken by another person since the spring of 1723, when Foucquet asked him if he would not change his mind and come to Rome. The speaker is a tall, dark man. His accent is foreign, but he knows the Cantonese dialect.

The man is Tonkinese, and he's been brought along to Charenton by the papal nuncio, whose furniture Hu rearranged one morning almost three years ago. It's only a fluke that the Tonkinese knows Chinese. He is a convert of the Augustinian missionary Roberto Barrozzi, and when Barrozzi was recalled from Tonkin to Europe they spent almost a year living in Canton while they waited for their passage to France, and the Tonkinese used the time to learn Chinese. Living in Paris for a while, the Tonkinese quickly picked up French as well. When someone on the nuncio's staff heard about this trilingual man from Barrozzi, they informed the nuncio, who was reminded of the injunction of the cardinals two years before to check on Hu's mental state at intervals. Now he can speak to Hu in person, at only one remove, and judge for himself.

When visited by the nuncio, Hu is voluble, but he concentrates on one main point: Foucquet owes him money. They made an agreement, the two of them, and Foucquet has not kept it. Hu should have been getting twenty taels a year and he's received nothing. Foucquet must pay what he owes.

The Tonkinese interpreter does his best to relay Hu's words, though he does not catch them all. The nuncio registers the fact that Foucquet owes Hu money. The nuncio is also interested in the story he's just been told by the prior, that Hu shredded a nice warm blanket. "Why would you do a thing like that?" he asks through the interpreter. "The blanket was mine to shred," replies Hu, "because it was given to me." Before the visitors leave, Hu scrawls a letter to Foucquet, asking when Foucquet will come back to Paris. Hu gives the letter to the Tonkinese, apparently believing that he will deliver it to Rome.

The nuncio thinks Hu may be sane. He decides to make inquiries about boat sailings, either from St. Malo, Port Louis, or Ostend, in accordance with the Roman cardinals' ruling of two years before that they would pay the fare for such a journey. It seems to him only fair that if Foucquet *does* owe Hu money, he should provide funds both to clothe Hu decently and to pay his way to his hometown once he's landed safely in Canton. The nuncio decides to write to Foucquet suggesting this. In the general confusion, Hu's own letter gets lost.

MONDAY, 24 SEPTEMBER 1725.
ROME, PARIS, CHARENTON

The nuncio's letter reaches Foucquet at the end of August, and Foucquet replies at once: Hu has never done the work for him agreed in the contract. Hu has been, consistently, a disappointment, and has no right to ask for his twenty taels a year. "If John Hu demanded a sum of money as his wages, then that proves that he has not regained his sanity."

The logic of this position is impeccable to Foucquet, but he does not ignore the implicit promise in the nuncio's letter that he will ship Hu home anyway, if Foucquet comes up with the money. Foucquet does not have much spare cash, despite his having recently been made a bishop. It is an honorific bishopric—his full title is now Jean-François Foucquet, Bishop of Eleutheropolis *in partibus infidelium*—in other words, there is no episcopal see, just the memory of former ones, now in the territories of Macedonia and Palestine. A Jesuit is forbidden by the Society's charter to accept such a title, but the newly elected Pope, Benedict XIII, has dispensed Foucquet from the vow he had taken as a young man to eschew all such honors.

Even before answering the nuncio, Foucquet has sent off a memorial to the Commission of Cardinals, headed still by Sacripante, that deals with Chinese matters. He reminds them of the existence of the "Chinese man-of-letters Giovanni Hu" who came to Europe to be his secretary and aide in translating Chinese books. He recalls the papal legate Mezzabarba's offer of employment to Hu in Rome should

Hu ever come there. He reminds them how Hu became mad, and how the papal nuncio graciously put the Chinese in a charity hospital. Lastly, Foucquet reminds the cardinals of their own generous action of September 1723 in voting funds for Hu, and suggests this beneficence could be repeated, with the addition now of funds for clothing Hu and for local travel expenses. "I humbly beg your eminences to deign to confer on this poor neophyte such a great act of charity," concludes Foucquet, "and the more so because up to this very hour the support of this man has cost the Sacred College of the Propaganda absolutely nothing."

By 5 September, the cardinals have decided to pay for Hu's return to China and any reasonable supplementary expenses. Having learned that Hu lives in Canton, they do not see the need for any further funds for him once he has landed. They so inform the nuncio in Paris.

The nuncio replies on 24 September, thanking Sacripante for his generosity. There are no boats leaving for China until January next year, so there is "plenty of time to orchestrate the departure of the said Chinese."

Hu is left where he is.

FRIDAY, 12 OCTOBER 1725.
CHARENTON

Father Goville has been brooding about John Hu for close to four years. He had not wanted Foucquet to take a Chinese assistant with him when he left for Europe, partly because he disagreed with many of Foucquet's religious interpretations of the Chinese classics, partly because Foucquet swung to the Sacred Congregation's position on the Chinese rites, and partly because of the possible legal ramifications and extortions of money from the Catholic community in Canton in case Hu should die while overseas. For those and perhaps other more personal reasons of active dislike of Foucquet, he tried to pressure the officers of the Compagnie des Indes, Bretesche and Tribert de Treville, into preventing the Chinese assistant from sailing.

After Hu's departure from Canton, Goville's worst fears were, on the whole, realized. Almost from the start, Hu's mother and brother began to badger the Canton Jesuits for money, assuming that since Foucquet had been a Jesuit, Goville shared the responsibility for their livelihood. Goville tried to deflect them by sending them to Father Perroni at the Sacred Congregation, since that was where Hu had worked and Perroni had abetted Hu's departure. Tensions with foreigners also increased after a Chinese boy, reaping in a rice field beside the Pearl River, was shot and killed by a British sailor firing from his longboat at a bird. This happened in October 1722, and Scattergood—who had been lucky to escape with his life in the accidental homicide of a year before—had to come up with two thousand taels in compensation, of which the bereaved family received three hundred fifty and the local officials the rest. There were still angry murmurs in the community about the affair.

Coincidentally, the situation of the mission in China began to change after Emperor Kangxi died in December 1722. His son Yongzheng cared nothing for the Europeans, nor their religion, and most were driven into a partial exile in Canton or Macao. The Jesuit influence in Peking was suddenly ended, and the whole tactic of conversion through ideological accommodation with the Chinese, which they had tried to follow since Matteo Ricci's mission of the late sixteenth century, was now called in question.

Goville returned to Europe on an English ship, the *Mon-*

tague, in 1724. He wrote to Foucquet while still on board, and posted the letter on landing in July, to bring him the dark news from China and to comment on Foucquet's views on the Chinese classics—"You hope to save the China mission by explaining the system of their canonical texts, this veil that so long hid the great mysteries of the true religion." Perhaps suspecting sarcasm or criticism here, Foucquet wrote in the margin of the letter that Goville didn't understand his views at all, but he answered courteously enough in late September, discussing the Chinese texts and Chinese politics, and asking for news of all the Fathers he had known in China. But Foucquet could not resist one parting jibe. At the end of his letter, after all the courtesies, he wrote (slightly misspelling the second name), "And send me, I beg you, any little news you may have of M. de la Bretesche and M. Triberd."

Goville replied on 5 November. He had been sick in Paris, and was recovering in the infirmary. He answered questions on all the Jesuits in China, but ignored the questions on Bretesche and Tribert de Treville. On 22 November, before Foucquet had had time to reply, Goville wrote to him on two other matters. One was a complex attempt to unravel Foucquet's book purchases and the accounting for them over many years. The other was the case of Hu, of which Goville had now clearly been given the details. Describing the fact that Hu's family had already been dunning the Jesuits for money, Goville asked what they would think when they heard of Hu's "malady" and what had happened to him. "His wife and children, will they leave us in peace? And if the Chinese does not return and ends up dying in France, won't they have a right to large sums of money in damages for the loss they have suffered?" The Chinese, especially the Cantonese, were litigious, said Goville. Look what had happened in the three recent cases in which Europeans had led to the deaths of Chinese. The results in each case were disastrous. Should not Foucquet prevail upon the Pope to send Hu home?

Foucquet, angry, answered on 2 January 1725. "Your worries strike me as excessive," he wrote. Without Goville's interference, he could have hired a Chinese who would have been "not only a great deal more suitable but would not have caused me all the trouble which that one did." How could the son Gaspar complain if his father, a grown man of forty, wished to strike off on an independent path? And Hu had no wife; she died long before. If the other three Chinese families got their money, that was because there had been violence involving guns and knives and even assaults on Chinese government personnel. In such cases, "a populace aroused by the sight of their compatriots' blood looked for vengeance and went to extreme measures. Mandarins have a right to punish foreigners who are brutal and rash." But in Hu's case, "since no one was guilty, why should the innocent suffer?" If Hu dies, could one "with any justice say he lost his life because of a European?" What sort of a general rule was Goville constructing here? "Are we now obliged to make all Chinese immortal if they take ship with us and travel with us to the kingdoms of the West? Who has ever thought of such a thing, even in China?"

Goville does not answer this sharp letter, and he does not act swiftly either. There is D'Argenson's prohibition on seeing Hu to circumvent, and there is a problem of timing. Goville gets to know Baynes. Through Baynes he learns that the prior of Charenton feels scruples that Hu still is not receiving the sacraments, and has not made his confession, because there is no priest to do it in Chinese. If Goville went to confess Hu, he could avoid D'Argenson's prohibition, but at the same time he would run into a second prohibition, that of the Archbishop of Paris, Cardinal de Noailles, who has forbidden the Jesuits to hear confessions in his see. Foucquet once received dispensation to confess Hu. Goville requests that prior Turpin of Charenton obtain another dispensation, so that he himself can come to Charenton. The prior obliges, and Goville makes the journey.

After Hu has told his tale and said his say, he asks his question, "Why have I been locked up?" Goville does not have the heart to answer that it was because they believed Hu mad. Because people were worried over the terrible grief you had shown when you thought your mother had died, Goville replies. Because they thought with Father Foucquet gone you would be alone in Paris, get lost again, and perhaps come to harm.

There is a little chapel for the pensioners in the room above the reception hall where Hu and Goville have been talking, among the other seated figures. The altar now is decorated with a glorious covering of red velvet and cloth of gold, fruit of the sale of the old Baron Leveneur's coat and waistcoat, and the five hundred francs besides that the Brothers of Charity voted to add to the five hundred which the sale of the clothes brought in.

Goville hears the confession of John Hu. Like Foucquet before him, he respects Hu's privacy, but he does not believe that Hu is mad. He thinks he is a Chinese man-of-letters who has been shamefully mistreated and deprived of his rightful wages. Goville would like Hu freed. He will not betray the secrets of the confessional, and he does not need to. He will just tell his friends in Paris the gist of what he has seen and heard, and let the rumor mill do the rest.

As Goville leaves, he tells Hu to write to Foucquet

again. This time Goville will make sure that the letter gets delivered. And Goville will tell Foucquet, in his own words, everything that Hu has just told him.

LETTER FROM HU TO FOUCQUET
WRITTEN BETWEEN 15 AND 30 OCTOBER 1725,
IN CHARENTON

"My respectful greetings to the one who receives this letter. I remember how we took ship and traveled together from Guangdong across the sea, for a period of a year or more, until we reached the capital city of Paris in the West. I committed no offenses whatever, and one can say I depended on the protection of God the Father. Nor did I shame you who brought me here. Everything went smoothly for me—it is hard to express even one-ten-thousandth part of my thanks.

"How could I have expected that a supervisor—a man I had never met before—let me stay in his building. I don't know where he heard it, yet he recklessly said that the Reverend Father [Foucquet] killed somebody, making me completely terrified, so that I suffered for many days. I declared my own innocence, but after I made my statement I was subjected to all kinds of further questioning.

"About fifty months or so after I arrived in the West I sent you a letter, entrusting it to a tall Chinese man who came to Sha-lang-dong [Charenton], so that he would send it by hand for you to read. I asked you to notify me of the date of your return. I don't know whether the letter reached you or not.

"Now it has just happened that my honored teacher Ge

[Goville] from the 'Clear Water Creek Church,' came on a visit to comfort me. He said that [you had seen] the Pope in the city of Rome, that all was well with you, and that you were thinking of going back to Guangdong via the West. I ask that . . .

[manuscript damaged]

. . . is near, and must not break your word, putting me in the position of being unable to look after my own family. Performing my worship, entering the church, hearing the Mass—all these things have been denied to me, and I fear I have greatly offended God and will not be able to atone for my guilt.

"Because he [Goville] asked about my situation just a short time ago, I am sending this message to you, hoping for your precious forgiveness. In all matters we should scrutinize ourselves, and act according to right principles. Please tell me your traveling plans as soon as possible, so as to stop me losing hope.

"I will say no more, but in all humility offer up this letter to you, Father Foucquet, whose saint's name is Francis, my honored teacher.

"From your Jiangxi disciple Hu Ruowang [John Hu], with homage."

THURSDAY, 15 NOVEMBER 1725.
ROME

It was a Monday night, 12 November, when Foucquet received the long letter in which Goville described his October meeting with Hu in Charenton. Foucquet was just leaving Cardinal Gualterio's country villa near Orvieto, where he had been a houseguest for several comfortable weeks. Reaching Rome on Wednesday night, Foucquet found Hu's own letter waiting for him.

Foucquet replies to Goville on Thursday morning, in a sustained twelve-page burst of fury. Hu's letter he dismisses as a daub of Chinese ideographs, as muddle-headed nonsense, as gibberish. But since Hu has added his own weight to Goville's implied condemnations of Foucquet's behavior, he will answer the points they make together.

The two of you raise three clusters of points, Foucquet writes. First, that Hu should, and wants to, go home. Second, that Hu is quite sane. Third, that I owe Hu money. As to the first, let Hu go, and as soon as possible, if he really will agree to go this time, and if the crew of an Ostend or any other boat will agree to take him after his past behavior on the way to Europe.

As to the second point, on Hu's sanity. To kowtow before a cross is acceptable in China, though three, four, or nine prostrations are the common norm—not Hu's private total of five. And his running through the streets of Paris? His mourning his mother when she was not dead? His horse in Port Louis, his knife-wielding, his smashing of Baynes's door? His preaching at St. Paul, his sleeping beneath open windows in winter, his cavorting in the sacristy of the Maison Professe, his walk in winter rain to Orléans? Ask Baynes, ask his daughter, about Hu's sanity. Ask the nuncio's staff.

And the third point? Foucquet owes Hu money? A contract is a contract. Hu refused to serve, whether from folly, from malignity, from indocility, from a spirit of rebellion—

which you choose is no matter. There are plenty of examples of each. Hu did nothing. Yet he got 10½ taels cash down in Canton. He had a lovely bed quilt. He got a grand suit of clothes in Port Louis. He got a carriage ride to Paris. He got food. He got the hundred francs given to Baynes. Why give any further explanations to such a man? Tell him he's mad, face to face, and have done with it.

Let the Sacred Congregation get the man his money and put him on a boat. But it was you, Goville, who by your meddling in Canton drove away the other Chinese who might have come with me, and left me this one.

I am, sincerely,
Yours, etc, etc.
Foucquet

SATURDAY, 5 DECEMBER 1725.
PARIS

There is a new lieutenant of police in Paris. His name is René Herault, and he has been in office less than three months. He hears the rumors almost at once. It is the job of the lieutenant of police to hear rumors and to put a stop to them. There seems to be a Chinese man in Charenton who should not be there.

Herault is extremely efficient. He is older than D'Argenson was when he had the post, but is still only thirty-four, the son of a wood merchant from Rouen. He has been married, widowed, and married again, both wives being the daughters of successful and politically powerful fathers. He has served in several major legal positions in both Paris and the provinces and is skilled at getting things done.

Herault finds that Hu has been incarcerated in Charenton on the authority of a *lettre de cachet* issued by his predecessor D'Argenson and Secretary of State Dubois. They promised to pay a pension in Hu's name from the King's treasury, but the money was never paid. D'Argenson has moved on to other things and Dubois has died. Herault acquires a countermanding *lettre de cachet* from the new secretary of state and sends it to prior Turpin at Charenton. Hu is released.

Herault puts Hu in a comfortable suite of rooms in Paris. He arranges for him to be washed and properly clothed. He tells the Royal Treasury to have the sum of eight hundred francs paid to help with Hu's return to China and to make up for the lost pension Hu was never paid. He asks the papal nuncio to move promptly to confirm a passage on one of the vessels of the Ostend Compagnie des Indes that will be leaving soon, in January.

Herault also arranges for a man to come to the apartment and teach Hu French.

WEDNESDAY, 16 JANUARY 1726.
PARIS

Hu has left Paris, rumbling north out of the city in the long-distance coach to Brussels. He will be staying there with another papal nuncio, Spinelli, before being transferred to Ostend and the waiting ship of the Ostend Compagnie des Indes on which his passage has been booked to Canton.

Since being released by orders of police lieutenant Herault, Hu has been behaving extremely badly. He refused to study his French lessons, and he made so many scenes in his apartment that Herault transferred him to the Paris nuncio Massei's residence. Hu behaved no better with Massei.

Massei has once more put his intendant, Marc Cardinali, in charge of Hu. The assignment seems logical in view of the two men's previous acquaintance. There is a definite passage for Hu on one of the Ostend vessels sailing in late January, and Cardinali has twice reserved a seat for Hu on the long-distance coach from Paris to Brussels so that he can get aboard early. Both times Hu refused to go at the last minute, and the deposit was forfeited.

This time Cardinali has taken Hu to the departure point, and brought a Jesuit Father along to help with translation and any other problems that might arise. When the coach is preparing to leave, Hu once more balks, and refuses to board it. Cardinali tries to push him inside the door, and Hu tears at his shirt. With a stronger push, and help from several of the assembled onlookers, Hu is thrust head foremost into the coach. As he tumbles in he lashes out with his feet, with one single well-aimed and accurate kick, at Cardinali's chest, pushing the man back several paces. There is only one other passenger booked on the coach. Cardinali asks him to keep an eye on Hu. Cardinali is not going to accompany Hu himself.

Recalling these events four years later, Cardinali wrote that he could no longer remember the name of the Jesuit Father who was a patient witness to these troubling events. Surely we know that it was Father Goville, interpreting with all his heart up to the last minute, interpreting until Hu was safely out of sight.

11

Return

Hu is back! The voyage was uneventful, and the three Ostend ships, sailing together, reached the Canton anchorage in October. They brought—along with Hu, and the goods and bullion needed for the China trade—bundles of letters for the Jesuit missionaries in Canton and Peking.

Hu goes at once to the mission house of the Sacred Congregation, where Father Perroni is still procurer-general. He demands money, the twenty taels a year promised for five years, that Foucquet never paid him. To calm him down, Perroni gives him something on account.

Hu greets his mother, and learns that she has received nothing but grudging handouts all the time that he was gone. He greets his son Gaspar, now a young man, who has been working with Perroni in the Canton church.

Hu stands outside the mission house and church of the Sacred Congregation—they have a new gatekeeper—and shouts out into the street. He shouts out to the Chinese strolling by until they stop to listen. He tells them of the journey he has made to Europe. He tells them of the rough usage that he received there. He tells them that he never received the wages that he had been promised as his right.

Hu is eloquent and tenacious. The crowds grow larger. Perroni says he will get the mandarins in and have Hu put away. Hu demands his money. Perroni persuades the captain of the Ostend ship, to whom Police Lieutenant Herault had ordered the King of France's gift entrusted, to yield up the balance.

The money is given to Hu. He goes shopping. He buys clothes as for a gala. With his mother and his son he sets off in his finery for his hometown not far away.

His son Gaspar cannot bear his father's posturing, and flees from him to seek shelter among other Christians in Macao.

Hu rests in his hometown, among the familiar sights and sounds. His son is gone, but sons do that. He still has his mother. Nobody living in Hu's hometown has traveled as he has. No one in Canton. No one in all the province of Guangdong.

Hu sits in the evening sun. He looks out at the drooping banyan trees, the rice fields now harvested and bare, the sluggish water of the familiar creeks, the barren lines of hills. "Uncle Hu, Uncle Hu!" the children cry, their eyes wide with expectation, their thin, confident voices rising echoless up into the sky. "Uncle Hu, tell us what it's like over there, in the West."

Hu pauses a moment, and closes his eyes.

"Well," says Hu, "it's like this."

Notes

xvi   The three manuscript copies of the *Récit Fidèle* are listed in the
       Bibliography under AAE; BAV, Borg Cin, 467; and BL, Add
       MSS 26817. A transcript of the AAE version, published by Henri
       Cordier in 1882, is listed under RF.

xvii   *Lettres Juives,* 1764, V, letter 147, 269–73. This particular volume
       is sardonically dedicated to Sancho Panza. The letter concerning
       Hu (his name is not given, though Foucquet's is) is intended to
       reveal abuses in the system of commitment by *lettre de cachet.*

xviii Voltaire, *Dictionnaire philosophique,* 1784 ed., section "Ana, anec-
       dotes," pp. 304–06.

1. The Question

12 OCTOBER 1725

3   Goville letter to Foucquet, 15 October 1725, BAV, Borg Cin,
       467, pp. 165–68, describing meeting with Hu the previous Fri-
       day, i.e., 12 October. Foucquet's own partial summary and cri-
       tique of this letter is in RF 541–47. On Goville, see Pfister no.
       258, and Dehergne, *Repertoire,* no. 382; and for his language abil-
       ity and the English in 1718, Morse, I, 158. Goville, in Borg Cin,
       467, p. 168, gives the romanization of Hu's question as *"so muen
       kin kinti,"* which in current pinyin would be "[*Weishema*] *suomen
       jinjindi.*"

2. Departure

30 SEPTEMBER 1721

5   Hiring of Hu, RF 384–85. This occurred three months before his first meeting with Foucquet—which was on 31 December 1721.

An excellent explanation of the function and structure of the Sacred Congregation—Propaganda Fidei—as it affected the China Mission is given by Witek, pp. 15–22.

On the range of churches and missionaries in Canton as of 1704, see Fontaney, "letter of 15 January, 1704," p. 324. Foucquet's count in 1721 was eight Catholic Fathers living in the city itself—two Jesuits, two Franciscans, one Augustinian, one Dominican, one at the Sacred Congregation, and one "D. D. Gallorum." Elsewhere in Guangdong Province he counted eighteen. Foucquet, "Catalogus Omnium Missionariorum," p. 69.

Hu's age, RF 529. Jiangxi ("Gan") provenance, Hu's letter, BAV, Borg Cin, 511, no. 5, line 24. Hu's mother and son, Gaspar, RF 551, 565. That Hu's wife had died long before (*"depuis longues années"*) is mentioned by Foucquet in a letter to Goville of 2 January 1725, BAV, Borg Cin, 467, p. 155. In the same letter he notes that Hu's son Gaspar was *"déja grand."* Living with mother, brother, son, see Foucquet's footnote, RF 538.

6   Hu's level of literacy can be gauged from his single surviving letter (in Chinese) to Foucquet of 30 (?) October 1725, BAV, Borg Cin, 511, item 5. That he had never passed any exams is specifically mentioned by Foucquet to Bignon, letter of 9 September 1722 written in Port Louis: *"Le Chinois qui a passé avec moi n'est pas un lettre du premier ordre, il n'est pas mesme gradué. Mais il écrit et il a lu toute sa vie."* BAV, Borg Lat, 565, p. 130 v.

For a letter getting misdirected on 10 August 1721, with serious consequences, because of the muddling of two different ideographs pronounced "Wang," see BAV, Borg Lat, 565, p. 103 v.

Gaspard (sometimes Kaspar, Gaspar) Castner (sometimes Kastner), Pfister no. 220, Dehergne no. 157, preached in Fatshan (Fo-shan) in 1700–01. Giovanni (Jean) Laureati, Pfister no. 221, Dehergne no. 451, was also preaching in Fatshan in 1700. Father Chavagnac wrote in 1701 of Castner's work in Fatshan: *"J'y trouvai un très-grand nombre de fervens Chrétiens, et ce Père devait, quelques jours après mon départ, baptiser trois cens Catéchumènes dans les Villages circonvoisins qui sont de son ressort"*—Chavagnac, p. 72. The dating of the conversion remains circumstantial, but since Hu was from this specific area, the coincidence seems too strong to ignore.

7   That Hu was definitely a catechist, and in the church of the Sacred Congregation, though never mentioned by Foucquet in RF, is revealed in his letter to Goville of 15 November 1725, pp. 180–81. Perroni confirms this in his letter of 10 January 1727, BAV, Borg Cin, 467, p. 127.

On activities of Canton catechists, see Fontaney, letter of 15 January 1704, pp. 322–23, on their shared confidences; Jacques, letter of 1 November 1722, pp. 191–92, on morning rounds; Gaubil (citing Father Baudory), letter of 4 November 1722 in *Lettres Edifiantes,* pp. 202–07; and Gaubil, ed. Simon, pp. 29–32, on hospital and baptismal procedures, and numbers baptized in 1719, 1721.

7–9   This description of Canton comes from two accounts of the city as it was in 1722 and 1723—Jacques, pp. 186–88, and Gaubil, ed. Simon, pp. 40–42 (the letter is misdated; it should read 1723, not 1722). See also the map, inserted following Gaubil, ed. Simon, p. 494, Planche II. On Whampoa, Dermigny, *La Chine,* I, 286. Other maps in Morse, II, 1 and 320.

10   The return of Fan to China, and the resultant memorials to Emperor Kangxi by the Canton region officials, can be found in *Kangxi hanwen zouzhe,* VIII, 701–02. The governor-general reports that Fan is "writing out in person a report of the events that occurred in Europe [*"xiyang"*] during his years there," ibid., 711. This account, the *Shen jian lu,* was finished by 1721. See Fan's *Shen jian lu,* transcribed by Fang Hao, p. 856. An intermediate version of this report is printed in Rosso, pp. 332–34.

11   Hu and the Pope, RF 385.

6 OCTOBER 1721

Foucquet mentions the serious illness of 10 August to 6 October, which kept him from all writing, in a journal entry of 6 October 1721, BAV, Borg Lat, 565, p. 104 r. That he was near death he mentions in a letter to Goville, Rome, 7 December 1724, BAV, Borg Cin, 467, p. 141. Given these indications, perhaps the crucial letter to Mezzabarba on the Rome journey, listed as written on 4 October 1721 (Witek, p. 376), should be dated 9 October. In BAV, Borg Lat, 565, p. 104 v, recording a conversation with Ciru, Foucquet mentions having received an answer to his letter of the 9th from the legate. In ibid., p. 117 v, letter to Menezes of 30 May 1722, Foucquet discusses his serious illness in Jiangxi, en route to Canton, in what I take to be *"Chiuchiang"* (the word is hard to decipher and could also be *"Chinchiang"*). For the example of his sense of aging and urgency, see the letter to Hervieu cited below, p. 184 v; "when one is fifty-seven" should be "in the fifty-seventh year." Foucquet was born in 1665, on March 12; see Witek, p. 75.

11–12   Biographical information, Witek, pp. 80–81, 169.

12   Hurried departure, Witek, pp. 242–43, and BL, Add MSS 26816, p. 144 v.

Private papers destroyed, BAV, Borg Cin, 467, pp. 183–84, letters by Dentrecolles and Bouvet. Ibid., pp. 164–65, on the figure of 1,200 Chinese books left behind, plus an unspecified additional number of European ones. In 1732, Foucquet told his visitor Joseph Spence that he "lost almost half of the collection I had made in the hurry of our coming away"—Spence, ed. Osborn, *Observations,* II (no. 1411), 524.

Canton 20 February arrival, BAV, Borg Lat, 565, p. 117 v.

13   Ships' movements, BAV, Borg Lat, 565, p. 117 v.

Book list, as in BL, Add MSS 20, 583A. See also Omont, pp. 810–11.

14   Doctrinal summary, Witek, p. 207, based on Foucquet MS letter of 26 October 1719 to Guibert. See also Witek, p. 155.

Foucquet to Hervieu, BL, Add MSS 26816, Canton, 1 June 1721, pp. 151–86. (On p. 186 he adds a note that this particular letter was never sent because of *"les dispositions dans lesquelles se trouvait alors le P. Hervieu."*) Hexagram 13, *"tongren,"* ibid., p. 166 v. No. 14, *"dayou,"* p. 170. Nos. 24 and 59, *"fu"* and *"huan,"* p. 171. "Reunion of all Peoples," p. 172. "Labor . . . sweet," p. 174. On these views, known as "Figurism," see not only Witek, *Controversial Ideas,* but also Mungello, *Curious land.*

15 Foucquet's copyists and secretaries, Witek, pp. 209–10. On Tartre banning their use in 1718, ibid., p. 236; Witek's bibliography of Foucquet's correspondence gives many references to such secretarial copies. Examples can be seen especially clearly, with the elegant Chinese calligraphy inserted, in BAV, Borg Lat, 566, the 906-page portmanteau volume of Foucquet's personal letters and his draft writings on the rites.

Two Chinese scholars, RF 384, with additional details on their coming to the Jesuit church in BAV, Borg Cin, 467, p. 154 (Foucquet to Goville, letter of 2 January 1725), and p. 180 (Foucquet to Goville, letter of 15 November 1725).

16 Early Chinese visitors to Europe are discussed by Dehergne and Fang Hao. For Shen Fu-tsung (Michael Shen), see Theodore Foss, "European Sojourn," and Thomas Hyde, ed. Gregory Sharpe, II, 516–20. For Arcadio Huang, see the descriptions in Elisseeff-Poisle, *Fréret,* pp. 41–50, and Knud Lundbaek, *T. S. Bayer,* pp. 87–88. For an imaginative analysis of Arcadio Huang, based on intimate knowledge of the sources, see Elisseeff, *Moi Arcade.* Fan Shouyi wrote the *Shen jian lu* to discuss his European trip. His arrival in Macao with Provana's corpse was reported to Kangxi at once—see *Kangxi hanwen zouzhe,* VIII, 701. A shorter version of Fan's travels is in his document printed in Rosso, pp. 332–34.

On Fan's trip to Peking and Manchuria, see Witek, pp. 240–42, and notes 226, 230. Foucquet mentions both Provana and De Lionne, along with Fontaney, Mezzabarba, and Maghalaens, and a "M. Bernard" and Ripa in his letter to Goville of 2 January 1725, BAV, Borg Cin, 467, p. 157. Witek, p. 244, n. 237, describes a dinner party on 18 May in Canton at which Foucquet, Mezzabarba, and Antoine Maghalaens were all together. It would be intriguing to know if they exchanged views on the usefulness of Chinese assistants. A full account of the legation is given by Sostegno Viani in *Istoria.*

Former Chinese emigrants returning to China were carefully reported to Emperor Kangxi at this time. See *Kangxi Hanwen zouzhe,* VIII, 828, for a 1721 report on 315 such returnees.

17 Perroni's visits on 4 and 13 December are in BAV, Borg Lat, 565, p. 107 r. Ibid., p. 106 v, shows Perroni had been with Mezzabarba in Macao.

Scattergood was the head trade officer or "supercargo" of the *Bonitta*. On this incident, see Morse, I, 168–69. The grisly precedent of 1689 is in ibid., 82–84.

17–18 The jailed three were Appiani, Borghese, and Guignes. See Rosso, pp. 187–88, Witek, p. 271, n. 54.

18 Foucquet's retreat, BAV, Borg Lat, 565, p. 107 r.

Example of Goville visit, BAV, Borg Lat, 565, p. 98 r (29 May).

18–19 Perroni friendship seems to date from later June, ibid., p. 99 v.

19 Foucquet wrote a long letter to Goville about the Chinese texts and his books on 4 August 1721. It is in BL, Add MSS 26816, pp. 144–50. The book titles and costs are in the Foucquet-Goville exchanges of 22 November 1724 and 2 January 1725, BAV, Borg Cin, 467, pp. 150–53 and 153–65. Both writers refer back to discussion in Canton during 1721. Biographical information (scanty) on Goville is in Pfister no. 258 and Dehergne no. 382.

20 For the most passionate statement of Foucquet's belief that Goville was responsible for deflecting the two scholars, see BAV, Borg Cin, 467, p. 154, beginning of letter of 2 January 1725 to Goville.

22 December date and Perroni—see RF, p. 384, *"douze ou quinze jours avant que les vaisseaux misent à la voile"* on 5 January 1722.

21 Study of the ships' locations and speed of *Prince de Conti*, BAV, Borg Lat, 565, pp. 117 v–118 r. Hope to be in France by May–June, ibid., p. 126 r, letter to Father Orry, 27 August 1722. Chinese on ships' movements, *Kangxi hanwen zouzhe*, VIII, 766, memorial of Kangxi 60/4/16 (11 May 1721), and 822, Kangxi 60 intercal. 6/16 (8 August 1721), which perhaps confuses one English and one French vessel. On the French privileges in China,

see Dermigny, I, 356. The references from the BAV archives below do not substantiate Dermigny's claim of *"desuetude"* for French privileges between 1720 and 1724. Morse, I, 252, on British; Dermigny, 1, 361, on their Nantes origin.

22 On Bretesche book purchases, BL, Add MSS 26816, Foucquet to Hervieu, 1 June 1721, pp. 182 v–183 v. Also Omont, p. 810, Foucquet to Bignon.

22–23 On Bretesche and Treville, the key references are all in BAV, Borg Lat, 565: p. 96 on Bretesche arrival (on the *Maure* or the *Prince de Conti*) and the silver; p. 100 r, translated Chinese terms; p. 101 r, dinner; p. 106 v, wine for Mass and discussion of St. John's Island (Sancian, Shangquan). Treville contacts with Hoppo and Foucquet, p. 106 r; books in cabins and Foucquet's need of them, p. 102 r.

23 Book freight charges in BAV, Borg Cin, 467, p. 152. The books were 268 francs (livres) 13 sous. The shipping costs pushed this "over 300 livres," i.e., totaled 31 francs or more.

Cabin profits for officers, Dermigny, I, 234.

31 DECEMBER 1721

23–24 The key supplement to RF 384–85 on the hiring of Hu is in BAV, Borg Lat, 565, Foucquet letter to the nuncio Massei of 3 October 1722, p. 144 r. This gives the details on the interview "5 to 6 days before leaving," the departure being 5 January 1722.

24 Foucquet's beard, which he won the right to keep even after arriving in Rome in 1725, was still impressive in 1739 when seen by De Brosses (Witek, pp. 315–16 and n. 160).

The details of French Jesuit dress in Canton—as of November 1722—are given by Father Jean-Baptiste Jacques, letter of 1 November 1722 to Abbé Raphaelis.

RF 541 gives Foucquet's sketch of Hu's hangdog look and physical dirtiness. RF 535 for Foucquet remark that Hu was *"baçané,"* dark-skinned. Foucquet's remarks on Hu's physical unattractiveness are made constantly in RF. Foucquet had spent the previous decade among the more slender, paler North Chinese.

25 Father Fioravanti reassured Foucquet that Gaspar was employed

by Perroni—BAV, Borg Cin, 467, p. 155, Foucquet to Goville, letter of 2 January 1725.

25 The contract and the purchases: RF 385, supplemented by BAV, Borg Cin, 467, p. 178, on the damask coverlet. Hu's refusal to keep his copy of the contract is attested by Goville, BAV, Borg Cin, 467, pp. 167–68.

A clear rephrasing of the contract and the food allowance is in RF 559, Foucquet's letter to Massei, 1730.

Mezzabarba's guarantee is discussed by Foucquet in BAV, Borg Lat, 565, p. 143 v.

25–26 Ibid., p. 144 r, Foucquet confusingly denies he promised to take Hu to Rome, though quoting Hu's "hope and desire." BAV, Borg Cin, 467, Pt. II, pp. 117–19, the permission letters are items A and B in Foucquet's appendix. Hu's desire to write up his travels and achieve fame on return is discussed by Foucquet at the end of his account, RF 552. Goville's legal arguments are in BAV, Borg Cin, 467, p. 151, letter to Foucquet of 22 November 1724, referring to cases that occurred before Goville had left China.

26 Goville's time in China, Pfister no. 258.

5 JANUARY 1722

Prince de Conti, crew size in RF 388, guns in BL, Add MSS 26817, p. 233; estimate of the ship's size, following tables and discussion in Dermigny, I, 203–07, 521.

27 Treville's letter is printed in RF 386, and in BAV, Borg Cin, 467, p. 185, the last letter in the third supplement to that copy of the *Récit Fidèle.* The letter should probably be dated 4 January, in view of Foucquet's 5 January departure.

Foucquet inventories his personal belongings in BAV, Borg Lat, 565, p. 157 v.

Cargoes: *Le Mercure,* for July 1722, pp. 174, 204, for the contents of the *Galatée* and the *Maure.*

Profits, Dermigny, I, 420–21.

28 Reorganization of company by John Law, see Dermigny, I, 155–56 and notes; Buffet, pp. 245–53, 261–63.

3. The Ocean Voyage

29 For the eight days becalmed, BAV, Borg Lat, 565, p. 112 r.

The barrenness of the delta hills was noted by many visitors, including Jacques, p. 186.

Witek, Bibliography, p. 377, lists some MS letters for 6, 8, and 10 January. Foucquet, BAV, Borg Lat, 565, p. 110 v, discusses making the fair copies, not far from Ling Teng (Lin Tin) Island on 13 January.

29–30 Hu's meal companions and habits are mentioned in RF 387. I am assuming these were his meal companions and habits early in the voyage as well as a little later.

30 Salaries for crewmen are in Buffet, p. 87. Numbers and salaries of adjunct officers, Dermigny, I, 222, 233. The French ships were heavily over-officered—as much as 39 percent of the complement were so ranked in some exceptional eighteenth-century cases (Dermigny, I, 222, table).

Macao date, BAV, Borg Lat, 565, p. 118 r.

Foucquet on voyage, *"nous eusmes la plus heureuse navigation jusqu'au Pol Condor,"* in BAV, Borg Lat, 565, p. 112 r.

31 Hu's seasickness, RF 387.

Gaubil, ed. Simon, p. 24, for their 22 January arrival.

Contemporary plans of the island can be found in Jacques facing p. 177, Gaubil, ed. Simon, facing p. 494.

Gaubil on the island, p. 10, repeated p. 18. (This letter cannot be dated 23 February 1722 as in Simon, ed., since it contains June 1722 astronomical observations. It should be Canton in late summer.) Jacques's view, p. 174.

32 Three married soldiers, Jacques, p. 176. Death of English, Jacques, p. 180, Gaubil, p. 19. Hostages taken, Jacques, p. 182.

French and German soldiers, Gaubil, p. 23. Decision to abandon island, Gaubil, p. 24. Poulo Condor as the earlier English port of call, Morse, I, 129, 135.

32 Jacques, p. 176, on the *Galatée*'s supplies.

Foucquet on the island, and his receipt of letters there, BAV, Borg Lat, 565, pp. 112 r, 188 r. His delivery of letters from Jacques and Gaubil is mentioned in ibid., p. 123 r.

Gaubil, p. 24, states clearly that January, *"le 25 au matin ces trois vaisseaux misent à la voile et ramenèrent en France la colonie."* Foucquet in BAV, Borg Lat, 565, p. 112 r says they left on 6 February. His recollection seems more likely to be accurate, especially given the time that would be needed to assemble the soldiers and settlers and close down the settlement.

32–33 Dermigny, I, 193–95, on the banning of the Dutch. BAV, Borg Lat, 565, p. 112 r, on hopes for gain.

5 MARCH 1722

33 BAV, Borg Lat, 565, p. 112 r, a close description by Foucquet, who clearly grew interested in these technical details of navigation, and p. 118 r. (Warp is *"touer"* in Foucquet.)

Hu's sickness, for two months from 5 January, in RF 387.

LATE MARCH 1722

34 Blows— *"quelques gourmades,"* RF 387.

The location is in accord with BAV, Borg Lat, 565, p. 112 r.

Hu's censorious views of the rough men aboard— *"la grossièreté des matelots et des soldats"*—is mentioned by Foucquet, RF 390.

Flogging, RF 387.

30 MARCH 1722

Foucquet description and date in BAV, Borg Lat, 565, p. 112 r.

General analysis of return voyages from China by the Cape of Good Hope in Dermigny, I, 263–64.

Loss of mast reemphasized in RF 388.

35 Missing St. Helena and the officers' conference, BAV, Borg Lat, 565, p. 112 r.

9 MAY 1722

A brief account of the battle is in RF 388, with major supplementary material in BAV, Borg Lat, 565, p. 112 v. Details on the *Prince de Conti*'s cannon, absent in those sources, are added in BL, Add MSS 26817, p. 233.

BAV, Borg Cin, 467, p. 7, confirms the *Prince de Conti* was hit by *"canon à Boulet."* Foucquet in RF 388 claims that Hu's action was a first proof of his growing madness.

36 On the harbor approaches, Frezier, p. 270, and Russell-Wood, pp. 43–44.

37 The general arguments on Brazilian landfalls are discussed by Dermigny, I, 250–51, and the precise months for 1719–69 given on p. 246. See especially p. 264, n. 4, where he observes of a Brazilian stopover for returning China traders, *"cette relâche ne se justiferait nullement au retour, alors qu'on continue à la pratiquer à l'aller."* The logic of this is further confirmed by the isochronic maps, Dermigny, IV, map 1. Frezier, p. 277, mentions that the big supply fleets used to come from Lisbon in March.

20 MAY 1722

For a panorama and description of the city at this time, see Frezier, pp. 272–79, and Russell-Wood, pp. 50–58.

The sailors' views of the joys of Brazilian landfalls, and Brazilian women, are given in Dermigny, I, 250–51, n. 8.

38 Witek, p. 255, and n. 6, Pfister no. 237, and Dehergne no. 96 for Belleville. Foucquet details his 13 May landing, the plight of his shipmates, his life with the Jesuit community in BAV, Borg Lat, 565, pp. 113 r and v and 122 r.

At the governor's request Foucquet wrote a lengthy account of his time in China, of the Mezzabarba legation and the presents sent to Portugal by Emperor Kangxi, and a brief summary of his own voyage; he kept a copy in ibid., pp. 114 r–122 r, delivering the fair copy to the governor on 30 May.

39　On the Jesuit church, now the cathedral of Bahia, which can be visited today, see also Frezier, p. 277; Santos, figs. 32 (for analysis of the ground plan) and 44; and Campiglia, pp. 20–24 and 37–47, which includes detailed photos of the sacristy.

31 MAY 1722

Departure date, BAV, Borg Lat, 565, p. 112 v. Foucquet says they were kept on the ship "14 to 15 days," presumably starting the count from 10 May.

Winter food and procurement problems in Frezier, p. 279.

LATE JULY 1722

40　The dating of the San Salvador stay follows BAV, Borg Lat, 565, p. 112 v. P. 122 v, which might have been expected to detail the departure and next stage of the Atlantic crossing, is left blank in the MS.

Hu's docility, his helpfulness on the ship, his dream, and his reaction to Foucquet's conversation, all in RF 389.

MID-AUGUST 1722

41　The La Coruña episode is in RF 388–89, supplemented by information Foucquet sent to Father Orry in a letter of 27 August 1722: BAV, Borg Lat, 565, p. 126 r.

In a marginal note in RF 388, Foucquet mentioned that the La Coruña governor was the Marquis de Ricbourg. Perhaps he was confusing the name with that of Burin de Ricquebourg, commandant in Port Louis when he landed.

There are numerous discussions of the 1721–22 Marseilles plague, which was a devastating one, in *Le Mercure*. Its ending was officially celebrated with a High Mass and "Te Deum" in Paris on 12 February 1723 (*Mercure* for February 1723, p. 380).

42　Foucquet to the Duc de la Force (*Lettres Edifiantes*, XVII, 73–128), Nanchang, Jiangxi, 26 November 1702. The madness episode appears on pp. 95–101. Father Chavagnac handled much of the case, but Foucquet states he was in the Jiangxi town of Fu-zhou when these events occurred in June and July, and followed the story with him.

42   RF 389, Foucquet, *"Je consolois dans l'espérance que la terre pourroit le remettre."*

43   Attempted Isle de Groix anchorage and escort to Port Louis, BAV, Borg Lat, 565, p. 123 r.

On Isle de Groix and smuggling practices, Dermigny, I, 238–39. On the armed Compagnie patrol boats—the *"pataches"*—Buffet, pp. 88–89, 94.

Port Louis harbor map, Buffet, pp. 394–95.

Letter to Father Orry, 27 August 1722, BAV, Borg Lat, 565, pp. 125 v–126 r. 27 August is certainly the date, though in Foucquet's hasty copy it looks more like 17.

4. Landfall

44   BAV, Borg Lat, 565, p. 123 r on officers and the director Lestobec.

44–46 Foucquet's letter to Bignon is in BN, MS Nouvelle Acq. Fr. 6556, pp. 103–104 v. Most of the letter is printed in Omont, pp. 810–11, with the missing section transcribed by Pinot, *Connaissance,* pp. 10–11 (the addressee is wrongly given as Fourmont). Neither Omont nor Pinot cites the left-hand marginal notation in BN 6556, p. 104 v, which shows that the letter, having been written on the boat, then had the return address corrected when Foucquet had been moved to Renault's home. An autograph copy is in BAV, Borg Lat, 565, p. 125 r. On Bignon's career, see Elisseeff-Poisle, pp. 31–33.

46   Renault and the *"canot du Roy,"* RF 390; Buffet, p. 94; BAV, Borg Lat, 565, p. 123 r. Confirmation that Renault was *"commissaire ordonnateur"* at that time is in Buffet, p. 93. The early voyage of the *Le Bon* is pieced together by the careful research of Witek,

p. 87. As this ship left in February 1698, technically it was not quite the twenty-five years before mentioned in RF 390.

47 Beating the retreat, Buffet, pp. 48–49.

29 AUGUST 1722

Renault's invitation, and Hu's living arrangements, RF 390. Foucquet collects Hu, and the book lists, BAV, Borg Lat, 565, p. 123 v. *"J'allai encore à Bord pour y chercher mon chinois,"* as Foucquet put it.

48 The *Galatée* arrived around 15 July—*Le Mercure* for July 1722, p. 174. The dispatch of the other seven crates is tracked in Omont, pp. 814–15. See also BAV, Borg Lat, 565, p. 129 r, in which Foucquet shows the books were on their way from the *Galatée* by early September 1722. Bignon (BN, MS Français 15195, p. 93 v) noted their final clearance by M. Guymont, presumably at Nantes, on 23 September in the evening— *"d'avant hier au soir,"* as he wrote on 25 September.

Hu and the housekeeper, RF 391.

1 SEPTEMBER 1722

49 The nature of Renault's work is derived from Buffet, pp. 90–94. Ibid., pp. 80–82, on choice of Port Louis residence.

On Ricquebourg and his son, Buffet, pp. 27, 94–96, 484.

Foucquet lists his new friends and the social whirl with pride in BAV, Borg Lat, 565, p. 123 v.

Bigot is in Buffet, p. 93; Martin du Parc in ibid., pp. 81 and 92.

Ricquebourg's quarrels with Parc, in early September 1722, in Buffet, p. 95.

50 The tailors and mocha coffee are in Buffet, pp. 275–76, 448. Color and type of suit and *justaucorps,* BAV, Borg Cin, 467, p. 178, letter to Goville of 15 November 1725. RF 400 notes that the suit was *"d'un drap fort fin et fort beau."*

Sketching the coaches— *"il griffonna les premiers carrosses qui se présentèrent à ses yeux"*—RF 552. On the poor state of the roads and the paucity of coaches, see Buffet, pp. 387–88, 399. Ibid., pp. 11–17, for general layout of the town.

Some hours of text copying in Port Louis, RF 535.

2 SEPTEMBER 1722

50   RF 390–91 for the ride, adding four days to Hu's arrival day of 29 August ("*il ne s'estoit pas ecoulé trois ou quatre jours depuis qu'on le eut amené chez M. Renaut* [sic]"). Buffet, pp. 397–98, on houses with *portes cochères*.

51   Streets of Port Louis, author's observation, and Buffet, pp. 393–94, 399 on eighteenth century. Wealthier men used carrying chairs to transport their womenfolk. Street map, Buffet, between pp. 394 and 395.

RF 391 on sending Hu home.

9 SEPTEMBER 1722

52   Foucquet estimate of Hu's five or six hours of work, RF 535.

The key 5 September Bignon letter and Foucquet's response are transcribed in BAV, Borg Lat, 565, pp. 129 v and 130 v.

52–53   The early growth of the Royal Library is meticulously charted in Omont, pp. 806–09. On Fourmont, see Lundbaek, pp. 88–89.

54   On Arcadio Huang and Bignon, Lundbaek, pp. 87–88.

15 SEPTEMBER 1722

Letter to Bignon of 14 September, Omont, pp. 811–12.

Abbé Jouin's odd goings-on are in Buffet, p. 68.

Petition to Company on damp books is mentioned in 11 September P. S. to Bignon, BAV, Borg Lat, 565, p. 131 r.

55   Poverty in Port Louis, Buffet, pp. 45–47, 87, 370–74. Night soil, p. 398.

Hu's insistence on begging, RF 392. Foucquet's interpretation of this, RF 552. On the new laws against vagrancy, see Robert Schwartz, *Policing the Poor*, pp. 29–31.

5. In the Provinces

56　The journey to Vannes and Hu's behavior, RF 392–93, 559. Foucquet rented a *"calèche."* I translate *"hoqueton"* as retainer.

57　Roads and countryside, author's observation, and the eighteenth-century "Cassini Map," sheet 6, covering the south Brittany coast.

Foucquet (RF 393) adds that the retainer spread the story all over Port Louis on his return.

The same day for the journey to Vannes, reached that same evening, is given by Foucquet in BAV, Borg Lat, 565, p. 131 r.

58　Vannes Cathedral, not a gem of architecture, gains its force from the way it rises above the maze of crowded streets that surround it so tightly. See the analysis by P. Thomas-Lacroix, *Le vieux Vannes,* pp. 16–22, and his admirable phrase *"sa masse trapue,"* p. 22.

College in Vannes, Delattre, V, cols. 16–18. Retreat, ibid., cols. 24–26, and quotation from col. 25, no. 1. For Goujet as rector, ibid., col. 20, and Goujet's warm welcome, BAV, Borg Lat, 565, p. 131 r.

59　Foucquet mentions the suit purchase briefly in RF 393, along with Hu's willingness to assist at Mass there. RF 400 emphasizes it was *"d'une étoffe assez grossière."* The fact that it was *"le frère couturier du collège de Vannes qui l'acheta"* is added as a marginal note in BL, Add MSS 26817, p. 235 v, and in BAV, Borg Cin, 467, p. 16. This confirms that these two manuscripts postdate the one in the Archives des Affaires Etrangères transcribed by Cordier in RF.

60　Letters forwarded on by Renault arrive 19 September. BAV, Borg Lat, 565, p. 131 v.

On Foucquet's general strategy, see Witek, pp. 256–58, and the bibliography of letters, p. 378. The letter to Bignon of 19 September was datelined Port Louis (BAV, Borg Lat, 565, pp. 138–39), but that was Foucquet's slip of the pen—he was already in

Vannes. The 19 September letter to Linières is correctly date-lined Vannes in Borg Lat.

60 Bignon picked up Foucquet's financial reasons for not going to Paris in his acknowledgment of 24 September: BAV, Borg Lat, 565, p. 127 r. And on the offer of Hu, Bignon wrote a special note to his colleague Fourmont, dated 25 September 1722. BN, MS Français 15195, p. 94.

5 OCTOBER 1722

61 Foucquet was told to work through M. Felonceau (sp?) in Nantes and had written to the commissioners back on 4 September. BAV, Borg Lat, 565, pp. 128 v–129 r, 131 r.

On the Sesines depot and the distance, see Omont, p. 815, and BN, MS Nouv. Acq. Fr. 6556, p. 110 r.

The struggle of the Jesuits to establish themselves in Nantes is finely told in Delattre, III, cols. 773–78, and the hydrography courses in cols. 784–85. Like the house in Vannes, they too ran a popular program of retreats.

62 Hu and Mass, women as reason, RF 393. On the complete absence of women from public view in Canton at this time, see Jacques, p. 188.

Bignon letter of 24 September 1722 is inserted (out of sequence) in BAV, Borg Lat, 565, p. 127 v.

Foucquet letter of 29 September 1722, Omont, pp. 812–13.

63 Foucquet to Nuncio Massei, 3 October 1722, BAV, Borg Lat, 565, pp. 143 v–144 v. I translate Foucquet's phrase *"écarts étranges"* as "outrageous behavior."

64 5 October, letter to Bodin, Witek, pp. 257–58 and n. 14.

5 October, letter to Nuncio Massei, BAV, Borg Lat, 565, p. 145 v.

20 OCTOBER 1722

Coach booking, Omont, p. 815, letter to Bignon of 15 October. In BAV, Borg Lat, 565, p. 158 r, Foucquet mentions he left Nantes on 22 October, reaching Tours on the 25th.

65 List of letters, Witek, Bibliography, pp. 379–80.

65 On Bignon's request, see Foucquet's letter of 12 October, Omont, p. 813.

Damage to crates and six journeys, Omont, pp. 814–15, and BN, MS Nouv. Acq. Fr. 6556, p. 110, letter of 15 October. This letter mentions four journeys already made to the Depot.

Linières to Foucquet, Bib. Ste. Geneviève, MS 1961, p. 9.

Undated Dubois letter to Linières about crates and D'Argenson, Bib. Ste. Geneviève, MS 1961, p. 9 v.

66 Foucquet preference for Loire route, BN, MS Nouv. Acq. Fr. 6556, p. 110 v.

Linières on Hu, Bib. Ste. Geneviève, MS 1961, p. 8 v. Nyel (Dehergne, *Repertoire*, no. 592) did not in fact go to China again.

Bodin permission, Witek, pp. 257–58 and n. 14.

Supervisor of the Nantes residence, Gilbert-Xavier Aumaître, Delattre, III, cols. 779 and 793.

67 Hu's kneeling cries, RF 393.

27 OCTOBER 1722

67–68 Hu's trip and inns, RF 394; Foucquet tried to seat Hu in *"les fonds."* Foucquet reemphasizes the windmill inspections in RF 552.

68 Foucquet, RF 394, charmingly calls Hu's way of warming himself *"cette impudente manoeuvre."*

Foucquet's rationalizations against taking Hu to the Maison Professe, RF 395.

Du Halde and Foucquet, Witek, p. 83; Foucquet's letter can be dated from RF 396. Du Halde later became a famous historian of China.

On Gramain and Foucquet's 30 October arrival, RF 395; Gramain as Orléans rector, Delattre, III, col. 1015. Gramain sending book money to Foucquet in China—at least 60 livres (francs)—is noted in BAV, Borg Cin, 467, pp. 161–62. RF 560, Foucquet called Gramain his *"intime ami."*

3 NOVEMBER 1722

69 Foucquet's departure and Hu's alarm, RF 397, 399. Since Foucquet arrived in Paris the night of the 3rd, departure from Orléans the night of the 2nd is assumed here.

For the two pictures in the Orléans Jesuit church, see Delattre, III, cols. 1007–1008. The unknown painter worked *"dans le goût de Vignon."*

6. Paris

25 NOVEMBER 1722

70 Hu's love of Paris, RF 398. King's first communion and Jesuit ballet, *Le Mercure*, August 1722, pp. 201–03, 164. Fireworks of 5–10 November, *Le Mercure*, November 1722, pp. 109–22.

71 Data on Baynes and daughter, RF 397, 402, and testimony of Marc Cardinali, RF 569. Extra 20 sous a day over minimum and size of rooms, RF 402.

Du Halde's level-headed views of Hu's problems are in his two letters of 30 October and 1 November, RF 396–97.

72–73 A basic source on the whole Maison Professe is Delattre, III, cols. 1259–1287. Germain Brice, II, 183–87, gives a good short description of the Maison Professe, and library, and 192–93 of the fountain. Other details are mainly from Louis Blond, *Maison Professe*, pp. 24–53, 77–89, 96–97. The great old days of the church are vividly described in Jacques Wilhelm, *Au Marais*, pp. 109–26. He lists the curiosities in ibid., p. 115.

73–74 On these aspects of the Marais that Hu could reach so easily on foot, see *Curiosítez de Paris*, I, 331, for the Louviers markets and the games of "Mail" at 8 sols each; 341, for the St. Paul river market and water coaches; 321 and 324 for Porte St. Antoine and the crossbow range; 324 for the view of the Charenton road. Also Germain Brice, II, 233, on Porte St. Antoine, and 241, on the Charenton road.

75 Du Halde and Nyel talks are in Witek, pp. 261–62. They cannot be dated exactly, but seem to have begun before the crisis with

the nuncio, or Foucquet would have been much more defensive. See his remarks on the delicacy of his position, RF 404.

76 Foucquet's travel plans are in RF 405. He states he began to make them on 4 November in Paris. Indeed, he would have gone straight from Port Louis if he could have cleared his books. Details on the official ending of the plague alert can be found in *Le Mercure*, July 1722, pp. 176, 206, and September 1722, pp. 52–64, 114–18.

77 Father Orry's helpfulness, RF 398–99.

27 NOVEMBER 1722

Hu's outing and disappearance, RF 398–99. D'Argenson's residence, *Curiositez*, I, 304, and Brice, I, map facing p. 1, building number 40.

78 For arrests of members of Cartouche's gang, see *Le Mercure*, June 1722, p. 140; July 1722, pp. 185–91; August 1722, pp. 220–23; and September 1722, p. 192. Williams, *Police of Paris*, pp. 66–84, gives an excellent picture of the whole Paris watch system, to which I am indebted. But the Guet activities traced here seem to contradict his conclusion on the desuetude of the Guet in the early eighteenth century, ibid., p. 70. *Curiositez*, I, 374–75, also gives a brief account of the Guet; and the broad range of their eighteenth-century activities is analyzed by Jean Chagniot, "Le Guet et la garde."

Saillant's extraordinary wager, and the role of the Guet and Cassini, *Le Mercure*, August 1722, pp. 197–99.

Venetian ambassadors and the Guet, *Le Mercure*, September 1722, p. 186.

28 NOVEMBER 1722

79 Hu is found, RF 398.

This list is drawn from the "Grande Police" hearing of Lieutenant D'Argenson, dated Tuesday, 15 December 1722, AN Y9423. The Grand Police review took place once or twice a month, Williams, pp. 28–36, and these would have been the people picked up in late November.

80 Nuncio's response, RF 399. His reason for wanting to see Hu in person, RF 400.

30 NOVEMBER 1722

80–81 Nuncio's audience, RF 400–01.

81 Nuncio's 9 October arrival in Paris, *Le Mercure*, October 1722, p. 156. His first audience, ibid., November 1722, p. 189.

EARLY DECEMBER 1722

82 Hu's dream of his mother's death, RF 402. The impact of Hu's grief was such that Goville heard all about it when he reached Paris two years later—BAV, Borg Cin, 467, p. 168, recalled in Goville's letter of 15 October 1725.

Room and broken door, RF 402–03. In RF 569, Marc Cardinali makes the startling claim that Hu *"voulant battre la fille de son hôte,"* Baynes in turn was *"obligé de le menacer et [le] battre avec un fouet, l'enfermer dans un cabinet et le garder à vue."*

83 Mass and sacristy episode, RF 401. There are many sources on the pomp and rather heavy majesty of the church of St. Louis, attached to the Maison Professe. Constans, *L'Eglise*, has fine illustrations. See also Brice, II, 170–86, highly critical of the church facade, and *Curiositez*, I, 307–12, plus the general summary by Blond, pp. 64–71.

On a personal visit to the sacristy in 1986, the author observed that the parquet floor, which seems to be the original seventeenth-century one, does indeed—to those who wish to see— present a complex pattern in interlocking crosses, because each square of hard wood is surrounded by thin, longer planks of differing length; thus it is logical, in a visual sense, to see each central block of parquet as containing one large central cross flanked by two smaller crosses, as at Calvary.

Rich food and begging, RF 402–03. In a caustic aside in RF 402, Foucquet notes that Hu certainly *did* eat better at the Baynes house than in China, where the typical diet was *"du riz cuit à l'eau, du thé grossier et des légumes assaisonnés avec une huile pestilente."*

LATE DECEMBER 1722

83   Books to Rouen, RF 405.

83–84   Hu's confession, RF 404. On the general Jesuit ban, and Linières, see Delattre, III, 1217–1218, 1276.

84–85   Hu's drum and flag, RF 403. A fine print of the old church of St. Paul, which was pulled down in 1799, is reproduced in Constans, *L'Eglise,* illus. no. 4. Hu's actions fit well into the picture of religious ecstasies and talking in tongues that B. R. Kreiser describes so vividly in his *Miracles, Convulsions and Ecclesiastical Politics.* For a view of the practices of 1730s ebullient Paris youth, see Robert Darnton's fine essay "Workers Revolt," in his *Great Cat Massacre.*

85   Foucquet's choice of words emphasizes his sense of furtiveness in the confiscation: *"par adresse, on enleva secrètement à Jean Hou* [John Hu] *sa bannière et son tambour,"* RF 403. The delicate Versailles negotiations are discussed by Witek, p. 259.

The fashionable congregation drawn to Linières's service in honor of "Madame," mother of the Regent d'Orlèans, is described in *Le Mercure,* January 1723, p. 192.

21 FEBRUARY 1723

Weather and Hu's disappearance, RF 406, which gives the date of Hu's departure as 12 or 13 February. In BL, Add MSS 26817, p. 241 v, Foucquet has corrected this to read "14 or 15."

86   D'Argenson to Foucquet on the books, note of 2 February stating they arrived Wednesday last (i.e., 27 January), is added as a marginal note to the *Récit Fidèle* in BL, Add MSS 26817, p. 241 v; this note is not in RF. Other negotiations on the books, Witek, p. 259, and the lengthy discussion on pp. 283–84, n. 89, which slightly confuses the issue of the original crates. Bignon's schemes are documented in his tough letters to Fourmont—see BN, MS Français 15195, p. 94 (25 September 1722); p. 95 (4 October 1722); and especially p. 97 (3 November 1722). The letter on p. 101 (25 March 1723), written a month after Hu's flight, is even more graphic: "Just be sure you keep his [Foucquet's] letter, which will serve as my title for demanding the books in question." On Fourmont, see the analysis in Lundbaek, *T. S. Bayer,* pp. 87–90, 104–06.

87 D'Argenson's letter in RF 406–407 to Foucquet, dated 23 February, says the orders to Duval are already given, but it seems neither Foucquet nor D'Argenson hurried this time. On Duval's career, see Williams, pp. 71–72, and his general discussion of inspectors, p. 95 (p. 101 has a fine table of their range of activities, but only for the period after 1750). Chagniot, "Le Guet," pp. 59–60, shows how well Duval was doing. For the range of Guet activities in late February, see *Le Mercure* for February 1723, especially pp. 379 and 382–90.

Those mentioned here and the others rounded up and presented at the "Grande Police" during this period are in AN Y9423, "Estat des Personnes" for 26 February 1723 (11 pp.). Gilles Lenoir is on p. 2—he had *"l'esprit aliienné."* The knife-wielding eleven-year-old, Pierre Laisne, is on pp. 6–7. Unfortunately, the entry is unfinished.

The schoolmaster, Claude Arme, was released on his wife's recognizance since she was able to prove he was a taxpayer (*"son Mary est à la Capitation"*), ibid., p. 2.

7. Orléans

20 FEBRUARY 1723

88–89 Gramain's letter is transcribed in full in RF, 407–08. Author's translation.

24 FEBRUARY 1723

89 Hu's impatience, RF 409.

Foucquet's letter in Chinese, RF 410.

90 Foucquet's apology to D'Argenson, RF 408.

Foucquet's house hunting, RF 409 and 415.

25 FEBRUARY 1723

Interpreter and Divine Providence, RF 410–11; the details on the interpreter's China service with Tournon are not in RF but are added as a marginal note in BL, Add MSS 26817, p. 244.

91 Shredded letter, RF 413, Gramain on 13 March referring back *"il y a quinze jours."*

91   In the emotion of reliving these days of separation, Foucquet in RF uses some of his harshest language about Hu, recalling *"la laideur de Chinois qui était extraordinaire"* (p. 410), and describing Hu as *"une des plus affreuses figures qui fut jamais sous le ciel"* (p. 411).

8 MARCH 1723

91–92   Gramain to Foucquet, 8 March 1723, RF 412. Author's translation.

12 MARCH 1723

92   Hu's meek worship or covered head, RF 413. In a marginal comment (not in RF) added in BL, Add MSS 26817, p. 265, Foucquet returns to this matter of the covered head in Orléans, and points out its significance in Chinese ritual.

93   Hu's moon viewing, RF 415.

Foucquet sends letter through Gramain, RF 411–12; asks Gramain to persuade Hu, RF 413–14. Hu's response, RF 415.

16 MARCH 1723

93–94   Detailed Gramain letter of 16 March 1723 on Hu's departure, RF 414. The printed RF account seems to imply that this one ticket on 16 March cost 12 francs (livres); but that this sum referred in fact to *both* the Orléans–Paris trips is explained by Foucquet in a marginal note, BL, Add MSS 26817, p. 246.

8. The Road to Charenton

28 MARCH 1723

95   Foucquet says Hu's room was *"dans le coin d'un des jubés qui sont sur l'église de Saint-Louis,"* RF 416; furniture, RF 419, Gaillard's permission, RF 417. The nuncio's intendant Cardinali called it *"un petit endroit près du Jubé de l'Eglise,"* RF 569.

On the church, see Martine Constans, *L'Eglise,* and Blond, *Maison Professe.* On the pictures, Wilhelm, *Au Marais,* p. 112. Three of the large paintings concerning St. Louis are still hanging in the transepts.

96   Foucquet's letters of 22 March and 28 March are not listed in

Witek, Bibliography, p. 381, and may well be lost. But that he wrote on those dates, and some of the content, can be reconstructed from BN, MS Français 15195, p. 104, Bignon to Fourmont, and p. 104 v, Bignon to Abbé Targny, both written 31 March 1723. See also Omont, p. 817, n. 1, though Omont, p. 816, mislabels Bignon's letter to Foucquet as being Foucquet's to Bignon.

96 Foucquet on first books to Marseilles, RF 417.

Hu in the streets, RF 416–17. It is hard not to see him as part of the pattern of that extraordinary Paris street scene of the early eighteenth century so well described by Robert Isherwood, "Entertainment," and Thomas Crow, *Painters,* pp. 45–54.

Renewed request to copy, RF 416.

Attempt to seize contract, RF 536, not dated but fitting the exact context of these remarks of Foucquet's.

8 APRIL 1723

97 RF 417–18 on preparations.

Shipment of the books to Marseilles can be confirmed as of 5 April 1723 by the letter in Italian of that date from the nuncio to Cardinal Sacripante, BAV, Borg Cin, 467, p. 119, item D (though by a clerical slip the date there is written as 5 April 1728). Translated French version is in RF 524.

Date of 8 April from RF 418— *"dans trois jours il faudrait se mettre en marche."*

10 APRIL 1723

97–98 RF 418–19 on all these details. Foucquet writes *"nulle représentation, nulle instance, nulle caresse, nulle crainte ne fut capable de fléchir sa folle opiniastreté,"* RF 418. For Hu's belief that Foucquet might have killed someone, an idea he implies came from a "supervisor," presumably Father Gaillard, see his letter of October 1725, below.

11 APRIL 1723

98 Eviction of Hu, RF 419. Foucquet adds that *"quelques autres personnes s'y trouvèrent aussi,"* but doesn't say who these were, or why

they were there: I take the lower figure of Foucquet's "two or three" Jesuits and "three or four *hommes forts.*" I assume the servants came from the large Maison Professe staff.

99 The inn, RF 420. The Hôtel de Sens is mentioned by name in Cardinali's testimony, RF 570. As the departure point for Lyon coaches, see *Curiositez,* 337. Cardinali's testimony, written in Paris on 27 March 1730, is an important addition to the story. Each of his statements bears the stamp of sincerity and accurate memory, but writing seven years later he conflated events that happened on three separate days—the 11th, 12th, and 15th—onto the one day of Foucquet's departure. This part of the story clearly relates to the 11th.

99–100 Letter to D'Argenson, RF 420–21. Author's translation.

101 Foucquet's packing, RF 420: *"obligé de finir quelques balots de livres et de hardes qui n'étoient pas encore en ordre."*

12 APRIL 1723

Foucquet on his departure and well-wishers, RF 421. Foucquet's *"anglois nommé M. Smihson"* (sic) is presumably the *"frère Smith"* mentioned by Baynes, RF 527.

Cardinali's account, RF 569–70, seems garbled, as mentioned above, and he confuses the Charenton departure for this departure. Hu was almost certainly left locked in his room—see Baynes, RF 526. Also Cardinali's remark to Foucquet—*"j'ai vu votre Révérence partir"*—carries the implication that he would have joined him if he could (RF 523). This is contradicted by Baynes's statement (RF 526) that Cardinali only joined him at home at five o'clock that morning.

102 For Foucquet's placing Hu in *"les fonds"* of the coaches, see RF 394.

The 100 francs were for future expenses, not past ones. Baynes had been paid in full for Hu's earlier expenses *"en pension,"* RF 422. The receipt is preserved in BAV, Borg Cin, 467, p. 119, as item C in Foucquet's annexe to his *Récit Fidèle.* It reads in full: *"Je recu des Reverend Père Foucquet la Some de cent livres pour l'usage du Chinois fait à Paris ce 12 Avril 1723."* Foucquet adds in a marginal note that this was Baynes's own spelling. That the receipt was written by Baynes right beside the coach is confirmed by Foucquet himself in BAV, Borg Cin, 467, p. 176 (letter of 15 November 1725 to Goville).

15 APRIL 1723

102–04   Baynes's account, RF 526–27. Cardinali's account, including Hu being tied up, RF 523–24, 569–70 (this latter telescoping several events). Papal nuncio's account, RF 525.

103   Role of Dubois confirmed in the anonymous letter of 11 February 1726, and Foucquet's ensuing comment, RF 550. There are many studies on the *lettre de cachet* system, so infamous in the *ancien régime*. A good summary of their procedural treatment in the police lieutenant–secretary of state relationship is in Williams, p. 42. Specific abuse of the *lettre de cachet* system in terms of commitment to Charenton is described by Mercier, *Tableau de Paris* (1733 ed.), XII, 35–37.

104   The important detail on the manacles was told to Goville by the prior of Charenton, BAV, Borg Cin, 467, p. 165: *"ce Chinois qui lui fut livré les menotes aux mains."* Foucquet responded acidly, *"Je ne scavois rien des menotes dont vous me parlez. Ceux qui les lui mirent eurent indubitablement des bonnes raisons d'en user ainsi"* (ibid., pp. 176–77).

Contemporary streets from Hôtel de Sens to Porte St. Antoine, Brice, I, folding map facing p. 1.

9. Inside Charenton

THURSDAY, 6 MAY 1723

105–07   Buildings, shape of courtyards, Esquirol map, plate xxvii. I was first led to Esquirol by the remarkable study of Michel Foucault, *Madness and Civilization.* See his description of Charenton and early treatment of the insane, pp. 42–43, 69–72. Mercier, *Tableau,* XII, 36, comments on how the Brothers of Charity betrayed their calling and became jailers by accepting those labeled insane in *lettres de cachet.* A good summary on Charenton is given by Marcel Gauchet and Gladys Swain, *La pratique,* and further detail on Esquirol's role is in P. Sevestre, "Eloge de la maison de Charenton." A bleak picture of contemporaneous treatment of the insane in Montpellier is given in Colin Jones, *Charity and Bienfaisance*, pp. 56–59.

107 The Brothers of Charity discussed the smells at their meeting of 14 August 1723: *"la mauvaise odeur des lieux communes du dortoir [?et] d'au dessus [?de] la salle des malades,"* AN, AJ2:84, Capitulaire of that date. The mending of the latrines was discussed at the meeting of 2 February 1722. There is no indication of whether the work got done or not. AN, AJ2:84, 2 February 1722, item 6.

On the continued unwholesomeness of these courts— *"vicieuse, défavorable au renouvellement de l'air"*—see Esquirol, p. 545.

Hu and mattress, RF 527. The prior's exact words, at least as reported by Baynes, were that Hu *"se tenoit toujours fort tranquillement dans son lit, et qu'il avait fait porter son matelas dans la cour pour lui faire prendre l'air."*

27 JULY 1723

A brief two pages of notes by Foucquet on this journey have been preserved in BAV, Borg Lat, 523, pp. 84 v–85 v, as indicated by Witek, p. 265, n. 36. It is mainly a list of expenses incurred, in cramped writing very difficult to read, and includes a notation on the 100 francs given to Baynes. On Foucquet's older sister, married to Antoine Guillaume d'Orbigny, Seigneur of Avallon, see Witek, p. 77.

Foucquet's papal audience, RF 528; Witek, p. 266, n. 39. Innocent XIII died not long afterward.

Meetings with cardinals and plans to petition, RF 528–29.

108 Worries over Baynes, RF 528; over Cardinali's report on the possible eviction of Hu, RF 529. "Giovanni Hu," BAV, Borg Cin, 467, pp. 120–21, annexe F, Italian version of the letter to the cardinals of which Foucquet's own French rendering is the one entered in RF. Here Foucquet uses "Gio" Hu, and the full name Giovanni in ibid., pp. 123–24, annexe I.

Foucquet not writing to Hu. See his rather lame excuse in the P.S. of his letter to Goville, BAV, Borg Cin, 467, p. 181.

On Foucquet in Rome generally at this time, and the Mezzabarba questions, see Witek, pp. 265–74.

108 The cardinals' 16 August probe of Foucquet's dealings with Mezzabarba is preserved in the remarkable document that has ended up in the British Library, the "Risposte date dal. P. Gio. Francesco Foucquet," BL, Add MSS 26817, pp. 179–89.

109 Books' confiscation, Witek, p. 259, n. 21. The last of the books were released only after Dubois's death in August 1723. They reached Rome in November—Witek, p. 284, n. 89.

For the Foucquet–Linières clash, see Bib. Ste. Geneviève, MS 1961, pp. 10–15 v, quotations, pp. 11 v and 15, letters of 29 June and 27 July 1723.

110 On the new Chinese assistant, see Foucquet's own transcription of Marc Cardinali's letter of 19 July 1723 in RF 527: *"vous avez trouvé un jeune Chinois, qui vous remplace ce malheureux qui est resté ici à Charenton."* The letter in which Foucquet himself described this new Chinese has not, alas, been preserved. Who was this young Chinese? Most probably, he had been brought to Rome in the entourage of Cardinal Mezzabarba, who returned there by May 1723, a month before Foucquet (see Witek, p. 266). Mezzabarba was one of the seven men specifically mentioned by Foucquet, in his furious letter to Goville of 2 January 1725, as having brought Chinese with them to Europe. The others were Fontaney, Provana, Bernard, Maghalaens, Ripa, and Lionne. BAV, Borg Cin, 467, p. 157. (Provana had brought Fan Shouyi, and Lionne Arcadio Huang some years before. Ripa brought four Chinese to study in Naples, with a Chinese teacher, but this would have been a year later. Ripa and Foucquet certainly met in Rome in 1724—BAV, Borg Cin, 467, pp. 131 and 143.)

21 OCTOBER 1723

3,000 franc "tax," AN, AJ2: 84, Capitulaire of 2 February 1722, item 12.

Grants to poorhouse, ibid., Capitulaires of 4 January 1720; 6 April 1721; 8 December 1721; 28 June 1722; 14 February 1723; and 5 September 1723. Furnishings and silver, 26 August 1725.

110–11 Leaks and contractor trouble, ibid., Capitulaires of 5 March 1721 and 8 August 1720.

111 Reservoir and pumps, ibid., Capitulaires of 2 February 1722, item 6, and 14 February 1723.

111 Land and real estate deals, Capitulaires of 3 November 1719; 25 April 1720; and 24 October 1723. For leads into scores of other sources on these topics, see the full table of contents to AN, AJ2 in Jean Favier, *Les Archives Nationales, Etat Général des fonds*, II (Paris, 1978), 496–97.

Vines, trees, manure, AN, AJ2: 84, Capitulaires of 8 December 1721; 6 July 1723; 24 October 1723; and 3 June 1725.

Charenton agreements, ibid., Capitulaire of 25 October 1725; De Laurière legal battles, Capitulaire of 5 March 1721. Esquirol, p. 549, also comments on their incessant squabbling with Laurière.

Carré Le Jeune, Capitulaire of 18 February 1725 and the Robillards' Capitulaires of 24 June 1721 and 10 August 1724. The most massive of their real estate purchases—the purchase of a mansion at 16 rue St. Antoine from the Comte de Ferrière for 50,000 livres, which led to endless financial and practical problems—can be traced through the Capitulaires of 5 June 1724; 6 July 1724; 7 August 1724; 10 August 1724; and 19 December 1725.

112 Prior's visits, Capitulaire of 2 February 1722, item 5, *"autant pour les consoler que pour connoitre leur situation."* Esquirol, p. 551, mistakenly notes the visits as being once a week.

History of endowment, Esquirol, pp. 541–42; hospital, ibid., p. 547. The tantalizingly titled item in AN, AJ2: 87, *"Chronologie de faits intéressant l'histoire de l'hospice de Charenton, de 1646 à 1717,"* is alas only one brief part page of dates and comment on the 1641 charter, its 1717 renewal, the vigils held in 1676, and the dedication of the chapel in 1679.

Pensioners share quarters with Brothers, and billiard room, Esquirol, p. 548. Privileged access to garden, p. 547. For the startlingly pleasant possibilities available to the Marquis de Sade during his incarceration in Charenton, see Gilbert Lely, *Vie*, pp. 595–605, along with Peter Weiss's vision in *Marat-Sade*.

113 Costs of commitment to Charenton: general figures, Esquirol, p. 553. Details are in the *"Registres des actes Capitulaires (1719–1742),"* AN, AJ2: 84, Capitulaires of 5 November 1719; 25 April 1720; and 25 August 1720, all arranging for some kind of 6,000-

livre payments. Comparable Montpellier fees are presented in Colin Jones, *Charity,* pp. 58–59.

113 Bank drafts and notes of exchange occur in the Capitulaires of 25 August 1720, 14 May 1721, and 24 June 1721.

On Sainfray family arrangement, AN, AJ2: 84, Capitulaire of 5 November 1719. Jean Batiste agreed to pay 300 livres a year for general expenses and 150 for food and clothes, in cash.

Robillard, AN, AJ2: 84, Capitulaire of 24 June 1721. Such an example would of course be balanced off by a speedy death, such as that of Guillaume Seguiry—AN, AJ2: 84, 25 April 1720, 25 August 1720, 6 April 1721—who lived less than a year. In this case the Brothers returned some of the money to his widow. Extra fees are shown in the Capitulaires of 5 November 1719, 25 April 1720, and 25 August 1720.

Annual rates and relation to diet, AN, AJ2: 84, Capitulaire of 23 December 1724.

Leveneur's coat, AN AJ2: 84, 26 August 1725. It is my assumption that the coat was embroidered—it may, given Leveneur's rank, have been some kind of full court dress.

114 Prior, Baynes, and Manners's family, RF 526–27. In Foucquet's spelling, the name is "Mannours" and his brother the "count." In fact the Rutlands were earls, later dukes, and the Mannours referred to by Foucquet must be either the Charles or John Mannours declared illegitimate by Act of Parliament following the spectacular divorce and adultery case of 1666–70 between Lord Roos, later Earl and first Duke of Rutland, and his first wife, Anne Pierrepont. This tortuous case would take volumes to unravel. Basic sources are in *Calendar of State Papers,* Domestic Series, for the reigns of Charles II, James II, and William III, and *The Main Papers of the House of Lords.* An excellent summary of the entire case is given by Antonia Fraser in *The Weaker Vessel,* pp. 298–310. The Charenton lead given by Foucquet offers an intriguing follow-up to her conclusion that after 1699 these sad children "vanish from the pages of history" (p. 308). The extraordinary story is further complicated by the fact that on 23 January 1684 the Earl of Rutland formally took custody of a "lunatic," the orphaned son of his close friend Sir John Fortescue.

114   Baynes on the 40 francs (*"quatre pistoles"*), RF 527. Foucquet on Dubois, RF 550. Police Lieutenant Herault on the nonpayments, RF 547. Cardinali on Hu being cared for *"sans nous rien rechercher,"* RF 532. The almoner (successor to Lecomte?) told Goville the same thing in late 1725. BAV, Borg Cin, 467, p. 170.

Foucquet, cardinals, and papal nuncio's interpretation of his orders, RF 529–33; nuncio's quotation, p. 531; dating of nuncio's visit to Thursday, 21 October 1723, RF 532.

To his chagrin, Foucquet discovered later that Baynes had spent the money on the trips to Charenton, not on Hu himself (RF 534).

115   These minor misdoings of the Brothers are given in AN, AJ2: 84, Capitulaires of 2 February 1722 (items 10 and 11); 23 December 1724 (items 7 and 8); and 7 July 1726, passim, on clothes, watches, and snuffboxes, and roaming in the country.

Lecomte was voted out on 3 December 1724 for "lack of confidence" in him (Capitulaire of that date, AN, AJ2: 84), but a successor had not yet been found.

The "humiliation and suffering" is Goville's phrase, BAV, Borg Cin, 467, p. 170, letter of 30 October 1725. Little luxuries: dispensary, Capitulaire of 2 February 1722; shoes, Capitulaire of 23 December 1724; bath house, Esquirol, p. 546.

116   Foucquet's shock on hearing Hu received no *"linge,"* RF 534. The precise details on Hu's wardrobe are from Cardinali, RF 571, and are likely to be accurate since Cardinali probably packed up Hu's things for departure. Baynes on desire to help Hu, RF 527, letter of 10 May 1723.

Prior and sacraments, BAV, Borg Cin, 467, p. 165, Goville letter of 15 October 1725. This prior would have been Théophile Turpin, chosen on 21 May 1723–see Capitulaire of that day, AN, AJ2: 84.

22 OCTOBER 1723–9 AUGUST 1725

Abbé Rota, Hu *"revenu de toutes ses extravagances,"* RF 531. Cardinali, Hu *"quasi enragé,"* RF 533. Baynes spending all the money on the trips, RF 534.

116 Nuncio's caution appears in both his letters of 11 October 1723 and 13 December 1723 (RF 530–31, 533). Hu later confirmed to Goville that he and the nuncio could understand nothing of each other— *"sans pouvoir se faire entendre l'un à l'autre"*—BAV, Borg Cin, 467, p. 170, letter of 30 October 1725.

D'Argenson's prohibition, for which no precise reason was given—it may have been routine in *lettre de cachet* cases—was mentioned by Cardinali in his letter of 19 July 1723 (RF 527–28): *"personne ne peut lui parler sans la permission de M. D'Argenson."*

Search for interpreter, RF 533. Father Armand Nyel was in Paris some of this time (Dehergne, *Repertoire*, no. 592, and Bib. Ste. Geneviève, MS 1961, p. 8 v, Linières to Foucquet, letter of 10 October 1722). But with only four troubled years in Macao and China, some of it under arrest, Nyel probably was not at an interpreter's level.

116–18 The meticulous data on the cells are given by Esquirol, pp. 544–48, and are based on his own observations of the old buildings as a staff doctor in the hospital in the nineteenth century, before they were demolished to make way for the new "model hospital" of his dreams. The broken glazing in the rooms, AN, AJ2: 84, 2 February 1722, item 6. For analysis and illustrations of other housing for the insane at this time, see Grace Goldin, "Housing."

118 Time span ends with the nuncio's second visit, with Father Barrozzi; 1724 was a leap year, hence the extra day.

Shredding the blanket, RF 536; Foucquet was informed of this act by Barrozzi himself in 1725, as shown in the P.S. of Foucquet's letter to Goville, 15 November 1725 (BAV, Borg Cin, 467, p. 181).

10. Release

119 Tonkinese interpreter, Barrozzi, and nuncio, RF 534–35. Hu's response on the blanket, RF 536. Foucquet noted that the Tonkinese was dark, *"baçané,"* like Hu, and almost as ugly. I date this meeting to 10 August because in his letter to Foucquet of 13

August, the nuncio said he had seen Hu *"depuis peu."* Based on current usage, he would have mentioned the day if it was longer ago than three and said "yesterday" or "day before yesterday" if it was less. But the precise date is not given in the text. On Hu's still not understanding the nuncio, see BAV, Borg Cin, 467, p. 170.

120 Foucquet got to know both the Tonkinese and Barrozzi when they came to Rome later in the year. He gives a very favorable assessment of the Tonkinese—contrasting him sadly with Hu—since he brought much joy to Barrozzi, entered the priesthood, and returned to his homeland as a missionary. It was Foucquet's impression that the Tonkinese was not fluent in either French or Chinese but could handle simple conversations in both (RF 535).

24 SEPTEMBER 1725

121 Foucquet's response to the nuncio is wrongly dated 12 September in RF 536. The correct date of 2 September is given in BL, Add MSS 26817, p. 256.

On Foucquet and his bishopric, consecrated 25 March 1725, see RF 535 and the careful analysis of the Jesuit position and the dispensation in Witek, pp. 277–81. On Eleutheropolis as a see, ibid., p. 278, n. 79.

Foucquet's petition to the cardinals is not included in RF. It is given in full, however, in a French version, BL, Add MSS 26817, inserted as a supplementary page. The date of 31 August 1725 is written in the Italian original, which appears as item I in the documentary annexe, BAV, Borg Cin, 467, pp. 123–24, where Foucquet used the form "Giovanni Hu."

122 Foucquet seems to have temporarily misunderstood the nuncio's remark that he should pay for Hu to get home from Canton, as meaning he should pay for Hu to get from Charenton to the point of disembarkation, *"pour l'envoier au lieu de l'embarquement"* (BL, loc. cit., p. 257 v). The nuncio had in fact said *"pour le conduire du port chez lui,"* according to Foucquet's own rendering in RF 534.

Nuncio and no boats, RF 538. The original Italian version is in BAV, Borg Cin, 467, pp. 125–26, as annexe L.

12 OCTOBER 1725

123   For the general background on this period, see Witek, passim (Goville-Foucquet contacts are in Index, p. 486). On the latest European accidental homicide, Morse, I, 174–75. Rosso, Bontinck, Mungello, Pfister, and Dehergne (see Bibliography) all give useful material.

A brief Chinese account of the closing down of the Canton Catholic churches in Yongzheng's reign is in *Guangzhou Fuzhi, juan* 87, p. 2.

124–27   The material in this section is drawn mainly from the fascinating exchanges between Goville and Foucquet. The letters used here are all in BAV, Borg Cin, 467, pp. 129–82. They appear as follows:

pp. 129–31. Goville to Foucquet, 25 July 1724, on the *Montaigu* (sic).
pp. 132–35. Foucquet to Goville. Rome, 29–30 September 1724.
pp. 136–40. Goville to Foucquet. Paris, 5 November 1724.
pp. 140–42. Foucquet to Goville. Rome, 7 December 1724.
pp. 142–49. Foucquet to Goville. Rome, 20 December 1724.
pp. 150–53. Goville to Foucquet. Paris, 22 November 1724.
pp. 153–65. Foucquet to Goville. Rome, 2 January 1725.
pp. 165–69. Goville to Foucquet. Paris, 15 October 1725.
p. 170. Goville to Foucquet, enclosing letter from John Hu [Paris, 30 October 1725].
pp. 170–82. Foucquet to Goville. Rome, 15 November 1725. Foucquet's lengthy summary of Goville's major 15 October 1725 letter in RF 540–47 has many distortions and omissions.

15–30 OCTOBER 1725

127–28   Author's translation, which must be regarded as very tentative, given the garbled nature of the MS and the various damaged sections. That the otherwise apparently nonsensical phrase *"lao-ba-er"* (or *"lao palh"*) was Hu's private way of referring to the Pope is stated by Foucquet himself in BAV, Borg Cin, 467, p. 176. I also translate *"Gao Han-ren"* as "a tall Chinese," though it could certainly also be "a Chinese named Gao." The original

MS of Hu's letter, written in ink that has now faded to reddish brown, apparently with a fairly fine quill, on a sheet of coarse paper 54 cm. long and 23 cm. high, is preserved in a file of loose sheets of Chinese documents in the Vatican Library, BAV, Borg Cin, 511, no. 5. (I am indebted to Witek, p. 264, n. 32, for leading me to this source.)

128 Though Goville's cover note to Hu's letter is undated in BAV, Borg Cin, 467, p. 170, Foucquet remarks (ibid., p. 171) that it was written 30 October. If Goville had had the letter any earlier than 15 October, then he would surely have enclosed it with his letter to Foucquet of that date.

15 NOVEMBER 1725

129–30 Author's translated summary of Foucquet's letter in the group of letters exchanged with Goville that are appended after the annexe to the *Récit Fidèle,* BAV, Borg Cin, 467, pp. 170–82.

129 He calls Hu's letter *"barbouillée de charactères chinois," "le brouillon"* (both p. 171), and a *"grimoire"* (p. 176). The letter ends the exchange, and no reply from Goville (or Hu) is preserved.

5 DECEMBER 1725

130 On Herault's career, see Williams, *Police of Paris,* passim, and pp. 299–300. In 1726, Herault played an efficient part in supervising Voltaire's release from the Bastille—see Voltaire, *Correspondance,* ed. Besterman, I, 280–98.

It is possible that details on Herault's handling of the Hu case are in the Châtelet police archives; I have not been able to locate them. I date this section to 5 December following RF 547, where the news is received in Rome on 14 December (approx.).

The other details on Herault are from RF 547, where Foucquet links Herault's actions to the Goville visit (the nuncio or Barrozzi could also have started some rumors, of course), RF 549 and 570.

131 The 800-franc (livre) total is specified as coming from the nuncio by Cardinali, RF 570. Foucquet mentions it merely as *"une grosse aumône"* (RF 549, 565) coming from Herault. Perroni saw

it as coming direct from the King to the Ostend captain, to be held in account for Hu. BAV, Borg Cin, 467, p. 127.

16 JANUARY 1726

131   Brussels and Spinelli, RF 571.

Herault and Hu's misbehavior, RF 547 and 549.

132   Cardinali, Jesuit Father, and Hu's departure, RF 570.

11. Return

EARLY NOVEMBER 1726

133   The arrival of the fleet, still all together in late October, can be reconstructed from the letter of Gaubil, anxiously awaiting (in vain, it transpired) his astronomical instruments and technical books for the mission in Peking. See Gaubil, ed. Simon, p. 132 (added note to letter of 6 November 1726—allowing for two to four weeks for the news to have reached him); confirmed p. 133 (letter of 10 November 1726); and p. 138 (letter of 21 November 1726) acknowledging Souciet's letter of 11 December 1725 just received. Certain back-up information on Western ship arrivals can also be gleaned from Yongzheng Palace memorials, but these are no longer as detailed as they were for Kangxi's reign.

134   That Gaspar worked in the church of the Sacred Congregation was mentioned by Fioravanti when he saw Foucquet in Rome— "*un fils déja grand qui se trouvait dans l'église du P. Perroni,*" BAV, Borg Cin, 467, p. 155. The other homecoming information is from Perroni's Italian letter to Foucquet, Canton, 10 January 1727, BAV, Borg Cin, 467, pp. 127–28, parts of which are translated into French by Foucquet in RF 550–51, and quoted in Italian (accurately) in RF 565. The final lines are from my imagination, though Perroni wrote that Hu "*con quel denaro che riceve si pose in gala e in Novembre* [lit. IX^bre] *parti con sua famiglia per sua patria,*" and Perroni also wrote that Hu "*in strada avanti la nostra porta radunava i cinesi che passarano, raccontando la sua gita all' Europa, i strapazzi ch'aveva ricevuto, ed il torto di non dargli il denaro concertato*" (BAV, Borg Cin, 467, p. 128).

Bibliography

AAE. *Archives des Affaires Etrangères* [Foreign Policy Archives], Paris, Quai d'Orsay. MD (Mémoires et Documents), Chine 12, Affaires Religieuses 1724–1866, folio pp. 6–83v, former Saint-Simon collection's version of Foucquet's *Récit Fidèle*.

AN, AJ2:84. *Archives Nationales*, Paris, file AJ2:84 (formerly listed as FF15:84). "Registre des Actes Capitulaires de ce couvent et hôpital de Notre Dame de la Paix de la Charité de Charenton Saint Maurice, ordre de Saint Jean de Dieu, 1719–1742."

AN, Y9423. *Archives Nationales*, Paris, Series Y, Salle Clisson, "Châtelet de Paris et prévôté d'Île-de-France," XIV, Chambre de Police, "Estat des Personnes" 15 X^bre 1722 and 26 Fevrier 1723.

Anon. *Histoire de la vie et du procès du fameux Louis-Dominique Cartouche.* Paris, 1833.

BAV, Borg Cin 467. *Bibliotheca Apostolica Vaticana*, Collection "Borgia Cinese," number 467. Pp. 1–116, transcript of Foucquet's *Récit Fidèle*. Pp. 117–128, substantiating letters marked from A to N. Pp. 129–182, correspondence between Goville and Foucquet. Pp. 182–185, miscellaneous letters concerning Foucquet's books, and a copy of Treville's warning letter.

BAV, Borg Cin 511. Miscellaneous materials in Chinese. Item 5 is a letter by Hu Ruowang to Foucquet, 1 sheet, 54 cm. × 23 cm.

BAV, Borg Lat 523. Collection "Borgia Latino," number 523. Folio pp. 84–85 contains Foucquet's "Breve Diario" of events in April–June 1723.

BAV, Borg Lat 565. Collection "Borgia Latino," number 565, materials by Foucquet. Pp. 96–394v constitute Foucquet's Journal and Letterbook for the period May 1721 (Canton) to September 1728 (Rome). The leaves also have page numbers in Chinese, from 3 to 550.

BAV, Borg Lat 566. 906 folio pp. of Foucquet's personal papers, writings, and secretarial copies.

Bib. Ste. Geneviève, MS 1961. *Bibliothèque Ste. Geneviève,* Paris, Manuscript 1961 (Supplement H.f.4°), pp. 8–15. "Fouquet [sic], lettres sur la Chine. Ci-inclus des copies des lettres écrites par lui ou à lui adressées, qui vont jusqu'en 1726."

BL, Add Mss 20583A. British Library, London, Store Street Depository. "Catalogue des livres Chinois apportés de la Chine par le père Foucquet Jésuite en l'année 1722," 48 pp., folio pp. 1–25.

BL, Add Mss 26816. British Library, London, folio pp. 144–150, "Lettre du P. Foucquet au P. de Goville Supérieur des Jésuites François à Canton, le 4 Août 1721." Folio pp. 151–186, Foucquet to Hervieu, Canton, 1 June 1721. Folio pp. 189–206v, Foucquet reply to Goville and Goville's enclosure ref. Foucquet's hostility to Jesuits.

BL, Add Mss 26817. British Library, London, folio pp. 231–266, variant copy of Foucquet, *Récit Fidèle.*

Blond, Louis. *La maison professe des Jésuites de la Rue Saint-Antoine à Paris, 1580–1762.* Paris, 1956.

BN, MS Français 15195. *Bibliothèque Nationale,* Paris, "Lettres de Monsieur l'abbé Bignon," folio pp. 74–142.

BN, MS nouvelle Acq. Fr. 6556. *Bibliothèque Nationale,* Paris, "Lettres du P. Foucquet," folio pp. 103–115.

Bontinck, François. *La Lutte autour de la liturgie chinoise aux XVIIe et XVIIIe siècles.* Louvain, 1962.

Brice, Germain. *Nouvelle description de la ville de Paris et de tout ce qu'elle contient,* rev. ed. 4 vols. Paris, 1725.

Buffet, Henri-François. *Vie et société au Port-Louis, des origines à Napoléon III.* Rennes, 1972.

Campiglia, G. Oscar Oswaldo. *Igrejas do Brasil.* São Paulo, n.d.

Cassini Map. Frères Cassini, *Carte de la France,* 1789, sheet 6.

Chagniot, Jean. "Le Guet et la garde de Paris à la fin de l'ancien régime," *Revue d'Histoire moderne et contemporaine,* XX, 1973, 58–71.

Chavagnac, Emeric de. Letter of 30 December 1701, Chotcheou, to Père le Gobien. *Lettres édifiantes et curieuses.* Toulouse, 1810, vol. 17, pp. 63–73.

Constans, Martine. *L'Eglise Saint-Paul Saint-Louis de Paris.* Paris, 1977.

Cordier, Henri. "Documents inédits pour servir à l'histoire ecclésiastique de l'extrême-orient," 1, "Correspondance du Père Foucquet avec le cardinal Gualterio," *Revue de l'Extrême Orient,* 1 (1882), 16–51.

Cordier, Henri. See RF.

Crow, Thomas E. *Painters and Public Life in Eighteenth-Century Paris.* New Haven, Yale University Press, 1985.

Curiosite̓ de Paris, Les, by "M.L.R.," rev. ed. 2 vols. Paris, 1742.

Darnton, Robert. *The Great Cat Massacre and Other Episodes in French Cultural History.* New York, 1985.

Dehergne, Joseph. "Voyageurs chinois venus à Paris au temps de la marine à voile . . ." *Monumenta Serica, 23* (1964), 372–397.

Dehergne, Joseph. *Répertoire des Jésuites de Chine de 1552 à 1800.* Rome, 1973.

Delattre, Pierre. *Les établissements des Jésuites en France depuis quatre siècles.* 5 vols. Enghien, 1940–1957.

Dermigny, Louis. *La Chine et l'occident: le commerce à Canton au XVIII͏ᵉ siècle, 1719–1833.* 4 vols. Paris, 1964.

Elisseeff, Danielle. *Moi Arcade, Interprète chinois du roi-soleil.* Paris, 1985.

Elisseeff-Poisle, Danielle. *Nicolas Fréret (1688–1749): Reflexions d'un humaniste du XVIII͏ᵉ siècle sur la Chine.* Mémoires de l'institut des hautes études chinoises, vol. XI. Paris, n.d.

Esquirol, E. "Mémoire historique et statistique sur la maison royale de Charenton," in *Des maladies mentales considérées sous les rapports médical, hygienique et médico-légal.* 2 vols. Paris, 1838.

Fan Shouyi. *Shen jian lu* [Record of my personal observations], 1721, transcribed in Fang Hao, *Zhongguo Xitong shi,* pp. 855–62.

Fang Hao. *Zhongguo Xitong shi* [History of Sino-Western Relations]. 2 vols. Taipei, 1983.

Favier, Jean. *Les archives nationales, état général des fonds,* vol. 1. Paris, 1978.

Fontaney, Jean de. Letter of 15 January 1704, London, to Père de la Chaise. *Lettres édifiantes et curieuses.* Toulouse, 1810, vol. 17, pp. 266–360.

Foss, Theodore. "The European Sojourn of Philippe Couplet and Michael Shen Fu-tsung (1683–1692)," in Marcel van Nieuwenborgh, ed., *Philippe Couplet (1623–93), the Man Who Brought China to Europe.* Louvain, forthcoming.

Foucault, Michel, tr. Richard Howard. *Madness and Civilization, A History of Insanity in the Age of Reason.* New York, 1973.

Foucquet, Jean-François. "Catalogus Omnium Missionariorum...." transcribed by Henri Cordier in *Revue de l'Extrême Orient,* vol. 2, 1883, pp. 58–71, from BL, Add MSS 26818, folio pp. 159–176.

Foucquet, Jean-François. Letter of 26 November 1702, Nan-Tchang-Fou [Nanchang fu], to Duc de la Force, *Lettres édifiantes et curieuses.* Toulouse, 1810, vol. 17, pp. 73–128.

Foucquet, Jean-François. *Récit Fidèle de ce qui regarde le Chinois nommé Jean Hou....* See AAE; BL, Add MSS, 26817; BAV, Borg Cin 467; RF. (The three MSS of Foucquet all use the eighteenth-century rendering "Récit Fidelle.")

Foucquet, Jean-François. "Risposte date dal. P. Gio-Francesco Fouquet [sic] della Compagnia di Giesu," Propaganda Fidei, Monday, 16 August 1723, BL, Add MSS 26817, folio pp. 179–189.

Fraser, Antonia. *The Weaker Vessel.* New York, 1984.

Frezier, M. *Relation du voyage de la mer du sud aux côtes du Chily et du Perou, fait pendant les années 1712, 1713 et 1714.* Paris, 1716.

Gaubil, Antoine. *Correspondance de Pékin, 1722–1759,* ed. Renée Simon. Geneva, 1970.

Gaubil, Antoine. Letter of 4 November 1722, Canton, to Monseigneur de Nemond, *Lettres édifiantes et curieuses.* Toulouse, 1810, vol. 19, pp. 199–207.

Gauchet, Marcel, and Gladys Swain. *La pratique de l'esprit humain, l'institution et la révolution démocratique.* Paris, 1980.

Gernet, Jacques, tr. Janet Lloyd. *China and the Christian Impact, A Conflict of Cultures.* Cambridge University Press, 1985.

Goldin, Grace. "Housing the Insane: A History," *Medical and Health Annual, Encyclopaedia Britannica,* 1983, pp. 36–59.

Gongzhongdang Yongzhengchao zouzhe [Yongzheng-reign palace memorials from the Palace Museum], vols. 6 and 7, Taipei, covering years 1726–1728.

Grand Bureau des Pauvres de cette ville et Fauxbourgs de Paris [Registers of Paris poor-relief expenditures for 1721–1724]. Paris, 1725. (In *Bibliothèque Nationale,* Paris, BN, R 7580).

Guangzhou fuzhi [Gazetteer of Canton prefecture]. Taipei, 1966 reprint.

Hu Ruowang (Jean Hou, John Hu, Giovanni Hu), letter by. See BAV, Borg Cin 511.

Hyde, Thomas, ed. Gregory Sharpe. *Syntagma Dissertationum,* 2 vols. Oxford, 1767.

Isherwood, Robert M. "Entertainment in the Parisian Fairs in the Eighteenth Century," *Journal of Modern History, 53* (March 1981), 24–48.

Jacques, Jean-Baptiste Charles. Letter of 1 November 1722, Canton, to l'Abbé Raphaelis, *Lettres édifiantes et curieuses.* Toulouse, 1810, vol. 19, pp. 166–199.

Jones, Colin. *Charity and* Bienfaisance: *The Treatment of the Poor in the Montpellier Region, 1740–1815.* Cambridge University Press, 1982.

Kangxi chao hanwen zhupi zouzhe [Palace Memorials in Chinese Language from Emperor Kangxi's reign], vol. 8, 1717–1722. Beijing, 1985.

Kreiser, B. Robert. *Miracles, Convulsions, and Ecclesiastical Politics in Early Eighteenth-Century Paris.* Princeton University Press, 1978.

Lely, Gilbert. *Vie du marquis de Sade.* Paris, 1982.

Lettres juives, ou correspondance philosophique, historique et critique. The Hague, 1764, vol. 5, letter 147.

Lundbaek, Knud. *T. S. Bayer (1694–1738), Pioneer Sinologist.* Scandinavian Institute of Asian Studies Monographs no. 54. London and Malmö, 1986.

Mercier, L. S. *Tableau de Paris.* 12 vols. Amsterdam, 1783.

Mercure, Le [Mercure Galant, Mercure de France], monthly issues, 1722–1724.

Morse. Hosea Ballou. *The Chronicles of the East India Company Trading to China, 1635–1834.* 4 vols. Oxford, Clarendon Press, 1926.

Mungello, David E. *Curious Land: Jesuit Accommodation and the Origins of Sinology.* Studia Leibnitiana Supplementa, XXV, Stuttgart, 1985.

Omont, Henri. *Missions archéologiques françaises en orient aux XVIIe et XVIIIe siècles,* Pt. 2. Paris, 1902.

Pfister, Louis. *Notices biographiques et bibliographiques sur les Jésuites de l'ancienne mission de Chine, 1552–1773.* Shanghai, 1932, Variétés Sinologiques no. 59.

Pinot, Virgile. *Documents inédits relatifs à la connaissance de la Chine en France de 1685 à 1740.* Paris, 1932.

Porter, Roy. *A Social History of Madness: Stories of the Insane.* London, 1987.

RF. *Récit Fidèle de ce qui regarde le Chinois nommé Jean Hou que le P. Foucquet Jésuite amena de la Chine en France dans l'année 1722 . . . ,* transcribed by Henri Cordier, from the MS copy in the Archives des Affaires Etrangères, Paris. *Revue de l'Extrême Orient,* vol. 1, 1882, pp. 381–422, 523–571.

Rosso, Antonio Sisto. *Apostolic Legations to China of the Eighteenth Century.* South Pasadena, 1948.

Russell-Wood, A. J. R. *Fidalgos and Philanthropists: The Santa Casa da Misericordia of Bahia, 1550–1755.* London, 1968.

Santos, Paulo F. *O Barroco e o Jesuitico na Arquitetura do Brasil.* Rio de Janeiro, 1951.

Schwartz, Robert M. *Policing the Poor in Eighteenth-Century France,* Chapel Hill, University of North Carolina Press, 1988.

Sevestre, P. "Eloge de la maison de Charenton," *L'information Psychiatrique, 52:3* (1976), 361–69.

Spence, Joseph, ed. James M. Osborn. *Observations, Anecdotes and Characters of Books and Men.* Oxford, 1966.

Thomas-Lacroix, P. *Le vieux Vannes.* Vannes, 1975.

Viani, Sostegno. *Istoria delle cose operate nella China da Monsignor Gio. Ambrogio Mezzabarba.* Milan. 1739.

Voltaire (François Marie Arouet). "Anecdote singulière sur le père Fouquet [sic], ci-devant jésuite," in *Dictionnaire philosophique,* section "Ana, anecdotes," 1784 ed., pp. 304–306.

Voltaire. *The Complete Works,* vol. 85. *Correspondance,* I, 1704–1729. Ed. Theodore Besterman. Geneva, 1968.

Weiss, Peter, tr. Geoffrey Skelton. *The Persecution and Assassination of Jean-Paul Marat as performed by the inmates of the Asylum of Charenton under the direction of the Marquis de Sade.* New York, 1965.

Wilhelm, Jacques. *La vie quotidienne au Marais au XVII* siècle. Paris, 1966.

Williams, Alan. *The Police of Paris, 1718–1789.* Baton Rouge, Louisiana State University Press, 1979.

Witek, John W. *Controversial Ideas in China and in Europe: A Biography of Jean-François Foucquet, S.J. (1665–1741).* Rome, 1982.

Index

A NOTE ABOUT THE AUTHOR

Born in England in 1936, Jonathan D. Spence was educated at Winchester and Cambridge; he first came to America in 1959, and joined the Yale History Department in 1966. He is also the author of *Ts'ao Yin and the K'ang-hsi Emperor: Bondservant and Master* (1966), *To Change China: Western Advisors in China, 1620–1960* (1969), *Emperor of China: Self-Portrait of K'ang-hsi* (1974), *The Death of Woman Wang* (1978), *The Gate of Heavenly Peace* (1981)—which was named one of the best books of the year by *The New York Times Book Review,* and awarded the *Los Angeles Times* Book Prize for history—and *The Memory Palace of Matteo Ricci* (1984). Professor Spence is married to the artist Helen Alexander and they live in Woodbridge, Connecticut.

A NOTE ON THE TYPE

The text of this book was set in a digitized version of Fournier, a typeface originated by Pierre Simon Fournier *fils* (1712–1768). Coming from a family of typefounders, Fournier was an extraordinarily prolific designer both of typefaces and of typographic ornaments. He was also the author of the celebrated *Manuel typographique* (1764–1766). In addition, he was the first to attempt to work out the point system standardizing type measurement that is still in use internationally.

The cut of the typeface named for this remarkable man captures many of the aspects of his personality and period. Though it is elegant, it is also very legible.

Composed by Graphic Composition, Inc.,
Athens, Georgia.
Printed and bound by The Haddon Craftsmen, Inc.,
Scranton, Pennsylvania.
Designed by Julie Duquet.

天主則深難追贖祈因個情即及便呈

彌撒等事俱失恐未得罪

費親有缺　聖禮進堂伏聽

仰希　金諒凡事省察循理祈平

示行族統難失望可也不宣稟

上

傅罷德勵聖神　方濟各　無爺　座前

韻都堂晚生胡若望頓首